A HISTORY OF EASTHORPE, ESSEX

A HISTORY OF EASTHORPE, ESSEX

by A. R. WEST, M.A.(Cantab)

with illustrations
by Hazel West

A HISTORY OF EASTHORPE, ESSEX

CONTENTS		*Page No.*
INTRODUCTION		5
CHAPTER 1	Origins	7
CHAPTER 2	The Manor and the Hall	14
CHAPTER 3	The Church and Rectory	26
CHAPTER 4	The Badcocks farms	37
CHAPTER 5	Ancient farmsteads	46
	Easthorpe Green	
	Scotties	
	Hoggets	
	Canfields	
	Winterfloods	
CHAPTER 6	Three village houses, past and present	61
	'No Name' Public House	
	Well Cottage	
	Great Guildhouse	
CHAPTER 7	Demolished or decayed farms and cottages	70
	Hazells	
	Winnings	
	Flispes	
	Joyes	
	Peacocks	
	St. Johns Garden	
	Filcocks	
	Minor Holdings	
CHAPTER 8	Some other village inhabitants	86
CHAPTER 9	The surroundings of the parish	91
INDEX		99

ILLUSTRATIONS

	Page No.
Map of Easthorpe	4
View towards Messing	7
Easthorpe Street	9
Bell Cottage	11
Easthorpe Hall	14
Osborne Tombs	24
Easthorpe Church	26
Rev. George Bowles	35
Badcocks	37
Little Badcocks	41
Easthorpe Green	46
Scotties	49
Hoggets	52
Canfields	56
Winterfloods	58
The No Name	61
Well Cottage	64
Flispes	75
Joyes	79
Filcocks	82
Postell Pightle	92
Whitehouse	93
Little Birch Church	94

First published 1989

© A. R. West 1989

ISBN No. 0 9511844 0 7

Printed in Great Britain by Technique, (A. G. Leach and Co. Ltd.)
Technique House, Stockwell, Colchester, Essex CO1 1HP.

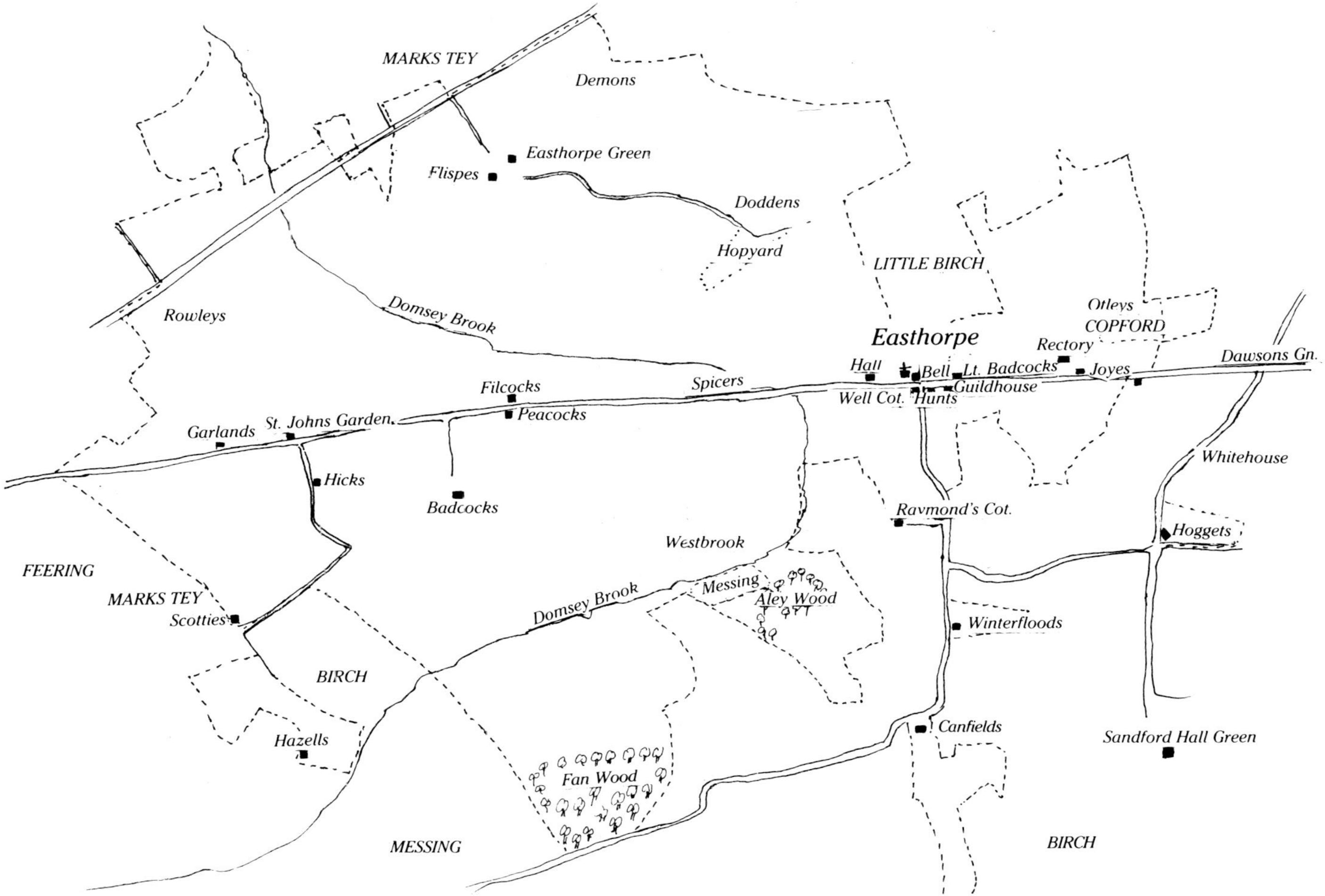
MARKS TEY
Demons
Easthorpe Green
Flispes
Doddens
Hopyard
LITTLE BIRCH
Rowleys
Domsey Brook
Otleys
COPFORD
Easthorpe
Rectory
Dawsons Gn.
Hall
Bell
Lt. Badcocks
Joyes
Guildhouse
Well Cot.
Hunts
Spicers
Filcocks
Peacocks
Garlands
St. Johns Garden
Hicks
Badcocks
Whitehouse
Raymond's Cot.
Hoggets
Westbrook
FEERING
MARKS TEY
Scotties
Messing
Aley Wood
Domsey Brook
Winterfloods
BIRCH
Canfields
Sandford Hall Green
Hazells
Fan Wood
MESSING
BIRCH

A HISTORY OF EASTHORPE, ESSEX

Introduction

This history of Easthorpe has its origins in my attempts to discover the history of my own house, Hoggets. The difficulties I experienced in doing so led me to extend my investigations further and further, beyond the boundaries of my own parish and even beyond those of the parishes adjoining.

I realised at an early stage that parish histories dealing in any depth with matters not of recent record are still uncommon. I can only suppose that this is not only because the interested amateur is conscious of his own deficiencies as an historian, as indeed am I, but also because he will seem never to come to the end of discovering new facts which elaborate or even slightly change the picture he has formed. As the picture is never complete, the history is never written. In my own case, it was finding the church terrier of 1637 in the Guildhall Library which at last brought me to realise that it had become my duty to record the various conclusions of my researches. That terrier is not in the Essex Record Office and I had believed it lost.

For the purposes of this history Easthorpe is defined as the ancient ecclesiastical parish of that name. What is more, although I appreciate that no parish is an island in itself, I have with the exception of the last chapter confined myself quite strictly to matters relating to Easthorpe alone unless they are of particular relevance or special interest. Nowadays the strange parish boundaries have been 'rationalised' for nearly a century, and the spiritual needs of what remains have been served from Copford for half as long. Administratively, too, this tiny parish is combined with Copford and has no separate existence. It is perhaps a little surprising that what is commonly considered as Easthorpe today is still very much what lay in the original parish plus a few houses around the four lane square from the church to Hoggets (a route known locally as 'round the island').

Easthorpe, however defined, is not a parish one would ideally choose for a parish history, and it is important that readers of this book should recognise what it lacks. It is, of course, much too small to provide any kind of microcosm of local social history or to serve as the basis for deductions and speculations about the district in general: its population rarely exceeded two hundred. What is worse, its records are sadly incomplete in several important respects. Such major sources as churchwardens' accounts and early manor records are almost entirely absent. There are, too, the particular difficulties arising from its boundaries, which lend themselves to no compact history; it is one of four local parishes whose detached parts are intermingled in a remarkable way. My attitude throughout has been that this is regrettable but has to be accepted. He who elects to write a history of his local parish has to put up with what he finds. The conclusion must be that if one day the history of every parish is written, some will inevitably appear much better or more interesting than others.

This history envisages as its audience the amateur local historian or curious local resident who wishes for a much more detailed account of the history of the parish than he will find elsewhere. I have included the history of all traceable dwellings in the

Introduction

parish other than those which are entirely modern. The parish has no houses at all which are of nineteenth or early twentieth century origin, and I have not been concerned to trace in detail the history of the houses I describe much later than 1850: this I leave to another writer. Although I believe that there is much in the history of Easthorpe which is of more than local interest, the general reader is bound to find in places an excess of local detail which he finds tedious; I have nevertheless included it for the purposes of record.

Tracing house histories in detail is a complex jigsaw, and I have put it together piece by piece over several years. The tortuous nature of its proceeding has led me to decide not to burden the text with references to sources, even though I am well aware that I shall be criticised for omitting them. In my view there are some areas of local history where the practice of noting every source document reference has become otiose and excessive. It has spread from academic scientific writing and at its worst has become a mindless habit. In the case of this parish history, which traces owners and occupiers in detail, yet where owner-occupiers are a rarity and few families remain more than two generations, I would have needed pages of notes to each chapter and in some instances three or four references to a sentence.

The references I have consulted are not remote and are readily available to the conscientious searcher. I have consulted all avowedly Easthorpe records in the Essex Record Office together with many of those of other nearby parishes. A few — a very few — references are to house deeds in private possession. I have made some use of material in the Public Record Office, but I retain the uneasy conviction that there are many illuminating references to Easthorpe which I have not discovered amongst its vast deposits. I have consulted all or most of the standard Essex reference books and histories and I have a particular debt to the Transactions of the Essex Archaeological Society, where some references are to be found to documents which I have not seen myself.

This parish history is a pioneer in North East Essex in that it is alone in attempting work of this detail. It is my sincere hope that others will follow and that these writers will find their task made just a little easier by what this book contains. When several more such histories do exist, I feel sure that it will be possible through wider vision to write a more general description of the social history of the district and to construct more enlightening accounts of the families who make brief appearances in these pages. When that can be done, this history will need re-writing.

I should like to thank my neighbour at Porters Green, Mrs. Diana Marriott, for her kindness in performing the difficult task of typing the text from my manuscript. I also wish to thank my wife Hazel, who has illustrated the book by sketches made in the field or from such old photographs as I have been able to discover.

A.R. West, M.A. *(Cantab)*

Chapter One
ORIGINS

Much of the parish of Easthorpe lies on a gentle southerly slope. This can be best appreciated from the stretch of street from Little Badcocks to the Rectory, where there is an attractive view to the low line of hills at Messing, a feature which represents the last and feeble vestige of the range extending from Brentwood and Danbury Ridge. Anciently, of course, and even recently, this view would have been hidden by forest or hedge, but the favourable and even slightly sheltered position of the village must together with the ready availability of a water supply have been a cause of its original siting.

The soil is chalky boulder clay, but most of the central part of the village stands on gravel, and this too may have influenced the first settlers. Claypits are frequently shown on old maps of surrounding parishes and are commonly referred to in field names, but they do not occur down the Easthorpe slope itself. There the small existing patches of woodland were once much more extensive; the straight field edges of later enclosure and the names of the fields themselves alike give clues to the earlier setting.

The only geographical feature of any significance is the Domsey Brook, which flows through the parish roughly west to east, turning sharply south at the Wash, just before the village centre, then for a short stretch westwards again. Its destination is the Blackwater. The name 'Domsey' is thought by Dr. Reaney to derive from a Walter Dolfin of Easthorpe mentioned in 1291 — a name which has Scandinavian origins. Although the Domsey Brook may appear to be a very modest watercourse of little importance, the difficulties it presented at the entrance to the village where it crosses the Roman Road — and which in wet seasons it still presents today, the road becoming impassable — are well remembered in the descriptive name of Slarvery Marsh given to the field it adjoins at that point. Its original course in this area has no doubt been changed. A little further on, near Well Cottage, there are several known underground springs, and along Well Lane these can overflow to meet with other waters seeking to reach the Domsey Brook to cause flooding of the lane for weeks on end. Further down the same lane, the name Winterfloods Farm serves to emphasize the problem.

View towards Messing

Apart from a hundred yard stretch of the present A12, once known locally as Domsey Lane and itself a Roman Road, the village is remarkable for having only two metalled roads. These are its street, of Roman origin, and Well Lane, a by-lane leading from the centre of the village to Messing. Although the road to the east of the parish was clearly once much wider than it is now, with eighteenth and nineteenth century enclosures of the wide verges allowing cottages on the manorial waste, this is no more than a common feature of the once heavily miry lanes in much of the county. What is

7

Origins

much more remarkable is that even the oldest village development clearly follows the line of the road both in Easthorpe village itself and, to the west, as far as the junction with the London Road. This strongly implies that although the Easthorpe Road was of obvious secondary importance to the Great or London Road, it did in fact continue in use well after the Roman period.

There are good grounds for believing that Stane Street is of earlier date than the Great Road, and the Easthorpe Road as a branch of the latter thus appears to be later still. Its original purpose, and indeed that part of its course which lies beyond the Gosbecks Temple site, at Cheshunt Field, is not clear and has been the subject of much speculation. It has often been assumed, on slender evidence, that is eventually enters the Balkerne Gate, but if it does so then it cannot be said to form any short cut: the distance from its junction with the Great Road is not less than if one continued to Colchester by the main road. It has also been suggested (by Miller Christy in the EAS Transactions) that it may have been constructed in response to some emergency such as the blocking of Stane Street, but it is difficult to imagine what sort of emergency can have prompted the construction of a smaller new road in preference to the clearance of so major an old one, to which indeed it runs so closely parallel. What is more, the Easthorpe Street runs through the marshy ground of the Wash, whereas to have branched off from a little further north would appear to have been much simpler.

Recent archaeological evidence has shown that Gosbecks was a much larger and more varied site than previously supposed; quite recently, too, an early fort has been discovered nearby. So much of the area remains unexcavated that such discoveries are unlikely to be at an end. In particular, it is suspected that it may have had pre-Roman significance. It is still safest to assume, therefore, that there was at some stage sufficient traffic from the London direction to justify the construction of a branch road to Gosbecks so as to avoid the nuisance of going into Colchester and back out again. As a road would also have led from Colchester itself to Gosbecks they would have appeared to form a single route; they would today indeed appear merely as an alternative way to Colchester if we underestimate the importance of Gosbecks. Another problem is why such a branch road did not set off from the junction of the Great Road and Stane Street, from which it is not far distant. Unless it was a pre-existing (Celtic) track the assumption must be that there was some obvious physical objection to doing so, such as thick forest as against cleared land on the route actually chosen.

There are some indications, referred to in several parts of this book, that land was cleared along the line of the road at some early period when forest still lay to the south. It may be relevant too that just to the east of the village and near the once substantial waste land of Dawsons Green, which is the crossing of the Easthorpe Road by the lane leading from Copford to Hardys Green, there are unexplained traces of early settlement including possible storage pits. Two Roman villa sites are known to be not so very far from the road — but the truth is that present knowledge is entirely inadequate to make any guess as to whether these or other factors played any part in determining its course. In this district of so many early remains finds of equal significance have been made in many localities which appear to have no Roman road connecting them with Colchester at all. In the case of the Easthorpe Road there has been little to encourage excavations along its route. Trial trenches at Dawsons Green found no trace of it, though its course at this point had been thought certain and just beyond its crossing

Origins

point of the Roman river at Gol Grove the embanked road is very clear. Recent chance digging suggests that it may have run just to the north of Dawsons Green rather than to the south.

The village which developed along the course of this road must be supposed, in the absence of any evidence of earlier settlement, to have had its beginnings at the time of its naming. If this is indeed so, however, then the continuance in use of this minor Roman road throughout the early Saxon period becomes even more remarkable. The only certain fact is that Easthorpe, the eastern dorf or village, is a recognisably Danish name, so that a late eighth or early ninth century date is probable. Not much is known of Danish settlements of that period in the district, nor are Danish names common in the county as a whole. Cleared land, on a south-facing slope, by a stream, and that not too far from the navigable Blackwater, would presumably have been attractive to settlers of the time, but not uniquely so. The really difficult question remains what it has always been: what is the east village east of?

Easthorpe Street

A number of answers to this conundrum have been suggested, though none is wholly satisfactory. The most usual explanation is Easthorpe's situation to the east of Kelvedon, which is an ancient settlement and which at one time had itself the name of Easterford or Estreford, and although this is not a particularly convincing idea, it remains the best available. Modern Easthorpe settlement, of course, lies to the east of the Domsey and for five hundred years at least has been heaviest in the most easterly part of the parish extent, but field boundaries implying early crofts make it possible that the distribution of population has not always been so marked. Again, Easthorpe may have lain in the east of some estate whose boundaries are unknown; but there is no evidence to favour such a suggestion and the force of Thorpe is generally of a secondary, not a main, settlement. All such theories can take a certain amount of illustrative colour from better documented or more easily proved cases of East or West villages elsewhere. At least it can be said that there is no suggestion of a Westhorpe, and in fact the generalised nature of the Thorpe suffix (as opposed to ham, in e.g. East Raynham

Origins

and West Raynham) would make it very unlikely that the village ever lay to the east of any other similarly named settlement. Careless of such considerations, local inhabitants till recently pronounced the name 'Eastup', but sadly this has died out.

The boundaries of the parish itself are unusual. They afford several clues to its history, but these clues are difficult to read. The shape of the main part of the parish is particularly strange, resembling a large balloon to the west of the Domsey Brook and a much smaller balloon to the east: the main settlement is at the point where these two balloons join. It is also remarkable that the ancient village inn, The Bell, which lies hardly more than a hundred yards from the church, was originally the southernmost tip of a large detached portion of Little Birch. In addition to these peculiarities the parish had a number of detached elements of about five to seven acres in extent, areas believed to be just about adequate in this part of the country for the subsistence of a medieval peasant family.

Detached parts of parishes are, of course, not unknown elsewhere. In Suffolk they are generally held to indicate an early fixing of parish boundaries and this may be so here, but it has to be said that no parish boundary in the vicinity has yet been positively identified as being established before the early tenth century. What can be said with certainty is that the extraordinary intermingling of detached parts of Easthorpe, the two Birches and Copford does not occur in surrounding parishes to anything like the same extent. The impression is given that these four were carved out of a single, pre-existing and more conventionally bounded parish, itself created some time earlier. If so, the mother or minster church can only have been Copford, where there is an undocumented tradition, mentioned by Morant, that there was once a nunnery and where foundations of unknown origin and date have been found in the grounds of the Hall. If, however, these detached parish portions are merely some kind of assart (woodland clearance) there is no guidance as to date: assarts are known to have continued in much of the county from early times until well into the thirteenth century.

Perhaps the most remarkable intermingling of boundaries occurs at Scotties, where not only does the boundary between Easthorpe and a small detached part of Marks Tey run through the house itself, but a detached portion of Great Birch is only a few yards away, and boundaries of Messing and Feering are not much further! The origins of this invite speculation. Perhaps the house, with its intriguing early name of Scotlives, was deliberately built on the site to confuse those who wished to establish parish obligations, or perhaps several parishes wished to lay claim to an important site: neither case can be proved.

More regular, and perhaps more significant, are the three detached portions of Easthorpe to the south of the parish church. Each of these is only a few acres in extent, and in each case a dwelling has certainly been on the site for four hundred years or so, with the obvious possibility of earlier dwellings still: these three are Winterfloods, Canfields and Hoggets. It is a reasonable explanation that each is an early holding deriving from an early clearance, and carefully retained within a local lordship at the time when parish boundaries were defined.

Winterfloods and Canfields lie against the winding lane from Easthorpe to Messing, while Hoggets lies on a lane connecting a remarkable series of greens within the distance of a couple of miles: Copford Green, Mulberry Green, Dawsons Green, Porters Green (where Hoggets stands), Sandfordhall Green, Hardys Green. On the land

Origins

between the two lanes the fields of Broadfield and Triggs appear from their large size and straight boundaries to be of later origin than the less regular fields higher up the slope and nearer the village. At other points near the greens various patches of woodland and known erstwhile manorial waste are clearly apparent.

A further but much more speculative piece of evidence about the extent of early cleared land lies between Broadfield and Easthorpe village, and this is the field known as Porch Field or Portwell. Manorial records even in the seventeenth century show a 2d fine paid for a porch although there is no evidence that any building ever abutted the field. In 1772, for example, the three daughters of William Stebbing acknowledge tenure of a "barn porch, formerly Thomas Stebbing's" but by this time it seems no more than a rationalisation of something everyone found puzzling. Porch field does, however, have a shape which is curiously angled at one point as though a gateway or entrance of some kind did at one time exist. This feature is adjacent to the glebe land just at a point where the parish boundary crosses an open field, and in the absence of any other explanation it is possible that the name may have derived from a form of the Latin portus, a gate. That this is not far-fetched is shown by the number of gates to the forest known elsewhere in the county: the many farms called Gate Farm seem often to have obtained their name from a similar origin.

Bell Cottage, once The Bell

In the parish register there is an interesting attempt to describe the more obscure parts of the parish boundary. It dates from 1630 and begins "This is only a note of such fields as are mingled in with other parishes". The idea appears to have been to clarify those instances where the parish boundary is not coincident with a field boundary, but although the areas to which the descriptions refer can be identified with some confidence on the tithe map it is hard to see what help they can have been on the ground. For example, there is nothing particularly definitive about "the nether end of a long croft against the road and a piece of meadow is in Easthorpe", even though it is clear that to the writer, as to us, "the road" was unmistakable. Elsewhere the account, which is in the rector's handwriting, makes great efforts to describe the nearly indescribable: "the upper end of the field called Damyes (Damyons) Field to the road is in Easthorpe, and from the east end of the same pond cross over the same field to a crab tree in a quick hedge about the middle of the same, and from here cross over the next field to an

Origins

oak on the other side of the hedge at the (word missed out) of the same field is in Easthorpe the oak not in the hedge but standing on the other side against the middle of the same". It is a lively illustration of the difficulties of determining tithable land.

Soon after this description was written the parish began to change its balance. The many ancient seven acre holdings ceased to be viable and were amalgamated with the other holdings, as the house histories given in this book describe, and with this change the population became rather more concentrated in the centre of the village. The tenements of earlier times were demolished or became labourers' cottages. Within the last century even these have disappeared. Today the centralisation of the parish population is more marked, although the size of the population has not much increased. Even so, most of the larger original farms remain.

It was mentioned earlier that the hall, the church, and a handful of existing old buildings and the sites of others lie at the point where the north and south parish boundaries of Easthorpe converge to such an extent that they almost meet. Despite its curious positioning, the village is classically centred on its Norman church and moated hall. The rectory, of mediaeval origin, lies some way further east, in the middle of the smaller 'balloon' of parish area. The glebe, similarly, lies near the rectory and never in the much larger part of the parish to the west of the hall, yet this easterly part is hardly more than ten per cent of the total parish area.

Examination of the field pattern shown on old maps — most notably and completely, the tithe map of 1841 — reveals many other interesting features. One which strikingly confirms the importance of "the road" and the antiquity of its course is the way in which the field pattern respects it as a dividing line: with one minor exception no field boundary lies opposite one on the other side. Ownership did not cross the boundary.

To the east of the church the field boundaries show no particular pattern. The fields themselves are in general somewhat smaller and squarer than in the rest of the parish and away from the road may be woodland enclosures. Around the rectory the pattern is confused and clearly much altered, reflecting the early dwellings and tracks referred to in the 1637 terrier. Beaumont Field, just north of the rectory, presumably relates to one or other of the two sixteenth and seventeenth century rectors of that name.

West of the church and south of the road the pattern is different. To the south of the Domsey Brook the field names unmistakably announce that they are woodland clearances. Bordering the brook itself are water meadows, their names similarly descriptive. As the brook bears away from the road there are on both sides of the lane small enclosures often named as crofts and looking distinctly mediaeval in size and shape. By the time their ownership can first be traced it may be significant that they are not generally owned in neat blocks, but several isolated tiny fields come together to make a single holding. Approaching Badcocks the pattern changes again, very large fields with related boundaries up to a hundred acres in extent having been divided at some later date, while small individual holdings such as Peacocks stand at the roadside. Other than these smallholdings the large fields were in the earlier eighteenth century of about twenty acres, though in some cases divided again later still.

North of the road the field boundaries are even more strongly related one to the other. One such curves gently field by field ever more north of west until it reaches the

Origins

present A12. To the south of this particular boundary later subdivisions are quite obvious. To the north the lane once known as Doddings or Doddens Lane runs from the A12 past Fouchers (Easthorpe Green) opening eventually into a field known for centuries as Grove Shot. Why Doddens Lane should have made so directly for this field is not certainly known, but there is no sign of it ever having continued further. It may have something to do with a mediaeval 'great field'. Three 'ley' and 'shot' names occur in close proximity here, and these are usually taken to be signs of mediaeval crop rotation and farming practice. What is more, some mysterious "lands of the towne called Dodwells" are referred to in the terrier of 1637, and this too is best explained as a reference to common land of mediaeval origin.

A few fields lie to the north of the A12 and here, in contrast to Easthorpe Street, some field boundaries do cross the road without regarding it. This is very remarkable, as it directly contradicts in respect of the Great Road what is so obvious for Easthorpe Street. It challenges the universally accepted idea that the Great Road was the major, and Easthorpe the minor, road at the time (whenever it was) that the field boundaries were fixed. Alternatively each may have a different origin. The contrast in the field boundary functions of these two Roman roads is too marked to be mere coincidence, and gives reason to suppose that there are traces here of some much older and underlying pattern of field or estate development which awaits elucidation. It is perhaps just one more example of how little is yet known of this part of Essex during the thousand years or so between Roman and Mediaeval times.

Chapter Two
THE MANOR AND THE HALL

The history of Easthorpe Manor can be derived from Morant, the notes of Holman, the researches of J.H. Round into its early history, and various stray references. The history of the Hall itself resembles that of any other of the village houses in that the story of its occupancy has to be assembled from isolated mentions in many different documents; as with so many other manors there has been no attempt to put the total picture together. One particular complication in the manorial history of Easthorpe is that it is frequently found 'going with Birch', as early writers assert. Birch in this context really means Great Birch, but the term 'Birch' is itself complicated by the three related manors of Great Birch, Little Birch and William a Birches, and they are often understandably confused in the records.

Easthorpe Hall

Of the three Birch manors William a Birches lay towards Layer and is rarely relevant to Easthorpe. Little Birch manor was based upon Little Birch Hall, but the mingling of the parish boundaries with Easthorpe and the frequency with which Easthorpe Manor was held by the resident of that hall, make for difficulties. Great Birch Manor is sometimes more problematic still. It was originally based upon Birch Castle held by the Gernons, but their name came to be transferred to the manor itself, often known as Gernons, or Garlands, and many farms or pieces of land in the area have that name or have it as an alias in old records. When this occurs, it can be construed as referring to an ancient manorial allegiance which does not square with later land ownership.

The Manor and the Hall

When Birch Castle ceased to be occupied, which is generally held to have been before 1300, Great Birch Manor changed its base and presumably its manor court to Great Birch Hall. This hall has long been forgotten in all records but its site was in fact at one end of what used to be known as Birch Heath, a stretch of land bordering the Maldon Road; its exact site is that of the present cottages which stand at the five-way junction where the Maldon Road is joined by the lane from Beckingham Hall. There may be some significance in there being a driveway between it and Little Birch Hall straight through the latter's park, but it is evident that Little Birch Hall, which even in mediaeval times ranked as an important residence, far outshone its neighbour. As early as the middle of the seventeenth century Great Birch Hall was referred to as Birch Hall tenement, distinguishing it from what was then simply called Birch Hall. For some now unknown reason the tenement and a small amount of adjoining land always went with White House Farm and Sandfordhall Farm or holding: the three together were always distinguished as being "of Great Birch Manor". Morant, writing long after this had come to be the case thus had the situation slightly wrong. He says that "the manor house stands two miles north west from the church, opposite Gernons, otherwise called the White House", but there is no evidence that any dwelling has ever stood opposite White House Farm, which is certainly meant.

The Manor of Easthorpe, though originally of less importance, outlasted both the Birches and its manorial court continued to sit into the eighteenth century. Its hall was, and is, in character mid-way between its two vanished Birch rivals, having neither the grandeur of the one nor the insignificance of the other. Its size and its position even today give the impression of a modest country house or large and prosperous farmhouse. The farmhouse image is accentuated by the barns which still adjoin it, the earliest being of the sixteenth century. The land in front of the barns used to be known locally as Pound Yard; this does indeed seem the most likely place for the manor pound, and a map of as late as 1741 shows a sketch of what looks very like a pound against the road. The land on which the Hall stands is moated, and one side of the moat separates it from the church. The house is set back a seemly but not excessive distance from the Roman road, and occupies the first slightly raised piece of ground to the east of Domsey Brook; until the present cottages were built no houses stood on the marshy ground between the two. The general impression is one of careful planning and positioning.

Of the Manor's Saxon or Saxo-Danish origins, nothing is known. Our first information is, as so often, the Doomsday Book entry. From it we learn that before the Conquest, Edric, a free man, had held the Manor, one hide and twenty five acres. The present holder was Eustace, Earl of Boulogne, with one Hugh as his under-tenant. The entry goes on: "then two bordars, now eight; then four serfs (servi), now two; then two carucates in demesne (i.e. in the lordship), now one; then one carucate amongst the men, now three; wood for thirty pigs, six acres of meadow; then one draught-horse; then worth forty solidii, now thirty". A slight fall in value of this order is fairly typical of surrounding manors.

The most striking point here is that the sharp increase in the number of bordars, or cottagers, was accompanied by a fall in the value of the property. The more independent style of farming does not seem to have led to greater prosperity. Each bordar would have had perhaps five to seven acres of his own, and it is interesting to see that several holdings of this size and apparently of early origin persist in the parish until late

The Manor and the Hall

in the seventeenth century. It appears likely, for example, that the detached parish sites of Winterfloods, Canfields and Hoggets have a long history and at least three others have a good claim. Indeed, if those ancient sites in the parish certainly attaching to other manors are excluded — e.g. Badcocks (independent manor), Hazells (Bourchiers Hall), Flispes (Bockingham Hall), etc. — then the remaining sites appear to match the Doomsday figures remarkably well, and may claim to be the most likely locations of the bordars' tenements. In the case of the detached sites a dwelling may well have been present when the parish boundaries were fixed, though it is of course a claim incapable of documentary proof. It should be noted, however, that if this is so then any smaller crofts to the west of Domsey Brook where, as stated earlier, old field boundaries imply that they may once have existed, were of an impermanent nature and a feature arising from the population increase of early mediaeval times.

It is not known with certainty who was the Hugh referred to in the Doomsday Book, though he was the under-tenant at Great Birch also. In the middle of the twelfth century the tenant was Hugh de St. Quintin, so the earlier Hugh may possibly have been his father. Not much can be said of these St. Quintins except that during the thirteenth century a family of that name were merchants living in or near Sudbury. At St. Gregory's, Sudbury, a fragment of Norman French inscription surrounding a lost brass still commemorates Seive de St. Quintin, widow of Robert; she died in 1300. This was not of the direct line of the Easthorpe family, however, for Rohaise, daughter of Hugh, married Roger de Planes and the lands were granted to them jointly at Hugh's death.

Roger de Planes must have inherited the manor between 1160-70. He had some involvement in a rebellion against Henry II and his land was taken into the King's hands while he himself laboured under the huge fine of £200 for what were described as offences against the forest laws. He was at that time one of those who favoured Henry's youngest son John, subsequently King but then Count, and continued his allegiance into the reign of Richard. He rose to high favour with John, becoming 'Justiciar for all the lands of Count John', but in 1191 he was killed in a London skirmish when John's followers encountered those of William de Longchamp as both were hastening to secure the Tower.

In 1198, still in the reign of Richard, there is a mysterious entry in the Pipe Rolls which shows that Birch and Easthorpe, now together worth twenty eight pounds, were held directly of the King by "Ibertus de Karenci". Nothing else seems to be known of him but, with John on the throne, by 1203 they were back in the hands of William de Planes, who in that year leased them to William Blund of London for three years, subsequently extended for a further three on payment of sixty pounds to the crown.

It was this William Blund who obtained from King John a curious privilege which has never been satisfactorily explained. He and his men, tenants of Birch and Easthorpe, were to be exempt of suits and shires and hundreds etc., and safely to trade throughout the King's dominions, paying the proper customs for their merchandise. From what is known of Birch and Easthorpe this can have had little practical utility as there was little merchandise to trade. Perhaps Blund had intentions for the area which were never realised; he had paid a good price for the lease in relation to the value, and his privilege was only for the term of that lease. Whatever his intentions, he seems to

The Manor and the Hall

have thought better of it because he assigned to Ralf Gernon his temporary interest — for twenty four pounds a year, payable in advance.

King John's reign saw the separation of England and Normandy after a series of military defeats, and those lords who did homage to the French king forfeited their English lands. Easthorpe was evidently amongst them. In the course of time such lands were deemed permanently forfeit, and it was then that Ralph Gernon obtained permanent possession. J.H. Round has shown (Transactions EAS, Volume XII) that this Ralph was the son of Osbert de Gladfen of Halstead. He was at one time in charge of Colchester Castle and he became the founder of Leighs or Lees Priory; he purchased a corrody and died old in 1248. The manor descended from him through William Gernon, Marshall of the King's Household, who also had the hundred of Lexden, then Sir Ralph, his son, who died in 1274.

Sir Ralph's son, Sir William Gernon, died in 1327. His was thus so very long a lordship that it is doubly regrettable that we know little or nothing of Easthorpe at that time. We do not even know for certain where he lived. Hardly anything is recorded of Birch Castle, which is always assumed to have been the usual residence of the Gernons, but it is known to have been the principal residence of Sir Ralph, William's father, who forfeited it to King Henry III. As there are no later records of its habitation, it is supposed that it fell into disrepair and was not inhabited thereafter, but if this is so it is not clear where the later Gernons did live. It is known that in 1265, when the Gernon estates were forfeited, they were taken into the hands of Sir Thomas de Clare, and it is also known that Peter Joye and Roger le Bover were keepers of the manor for the king until Sir Ralph received them back. Perhaps when he returned he lived at Great Birch Hall, or perhaps even at Easthorpe, though no shred of evidence supports any such supposition. A number of the architectural features of Easthorpe church do date from Sir Ralph's or Sir William's time and may therefore arise from their especial interest — but there again, they may not.

The next Gernon, Sir John, was the last. His elder daughter predeceased him, but his younger, Margaret, was married to Sir John Peyton of Peyton Hall, Boxford, so after the death of Sir John Gernon the manor passed to Sir John Peyton in right of his wife. For the next century and a half the history of the manor is no more than a dry recital of names of the Peytons, and who lived at the hall is quite unknown. Whether the Peytons took any particular interest in Easthorpe is doubtful, but it seems possible that they did; they carefully built up their landholdings in the surrounding district, and the hall was rebuilt in the late fifteenth century when they still owned the manor.

The succession of Peytons is detailed by Morant, and may be summarised as follows. Sir John was survived by his Gernon wife Margaret, their son John having died before her. Margaret died at a great age in 1414, and was succeeded by her grandson, another John. This John held the estate for only three years until his own death. His widow, Grace, was re-married to Richard Baynard of Messing, but the heir was the son of John and Grace, yet another John, born in the year of old Margaret's death. This John died when he was only eighteen, whereupon the estate passed to his brother Thomas. Sir Thomas had the distinction of being a longer-lived Peyton, becoming Sheriff of Cambridge and Huntingdon and surviving until 1484. His son, however, had predeceased him, and it was his grandson, another Thomas, who inherited. This second Sir Thomas lived only till 1490, however, and his younger brother, Robert, succeeded him. Sir Robert died in 1517, and was succeeded by his son, likewise called

The Manor and the Hall

Robert; from him it passed in turn to his son, yet another Robert, who in 1536 alienated the manor together with the hundred of Lexden. So ended the Peyton connection.

The new owner was none other than Sir Thomas Audeley, Lord Chancellor of England, a notoriously greedy collector of monastic and other property. Easthorpe must have been acquired almost unnoticed. Amongst his appropriations was Berechurch, which after his death passed to his nephew, another Thomas Audeley: it was this Thomas's wife, Katherine, who figures in the history of Badcocks (see Chapter 4). As part of the Lord Chancellor's wheeling and dealing he conveyed the manor and indeed the hundred to Richard Gresham only a couple of months later, who in turn conveyed them back to Audeley in July of the following year. The reason for this is not clear. Audeley held on to the manor for nearly five years on this second occasion, selling it to Richard Forster in October, 1542. By that time he was newly created Lord Audeley of Walden, but was in failing health and died eighteen months later.

The manor at this period went once again with Birch, and although Robert Forster himself was not a great landowner he was another in the long line of lords of Easthorpe who chose to reside outside the parish. In Forster's case that residence was Little Birch Hall, already referred to simply as Birch Hall. This he had inherited from his father-in-law in 1500, adding to his estate in 1523 further major purchases of land from Thomas Tey.

Robert Forster's will survives and is dated 25th November, 1555. The profits of the manor of Easthorpe Hall for ten years after his decease he leaves, in furtherance of an arrangement with his son George Forster and others, to the provision of an Easter Sepulchre in Little Birch Church. His words are "I wish that an gravestone be bought and layed over me in a place where they use to put the sepulchre and that it might serve instead of a sepulchre". This type of tomb was not uncommon at the time. Amongst his other bequests was one to his servant of his gelding, boots, spurs, saddles and bridles, also to his sons his "furre sarsen jacket and doublet and his cote corded with velvet".

It is unlikely that his wishes as to the sepulchre were fulfilled, since his will was proved in 1557 and the state religion in England changed almost immediately afterwards with the death of Mary. By a coincidence he died in the same year as John Kingston, rector of Easthorpe and latterly Great Birch, whom he must have known and whose will shows concerns of just this kind (and is described in the next chapter). As to George Forster, who succeeded, there is contradictory evidence. Morant states that he died on 4th November, 1555, but this would have been before the death of his father Robert, in whose will he was mentioned and of which in 1557 he was executor, and there is other evidence that George outlived his father. Morant's date is so precise however, that is is difficult to dismiss. Perhaps it refers to a brother or other close relation of Robert; in this case he may well have resided at Easthorpe Hall, of which Morant states George died possessed.

However this may be, the manor did in time pass to the heiresses of George the son. Mary, one of these, married Robert Waldegrave, but she seems to have been a girl of some spirit, as she soon ran off and "consoled herself" with a certain William Sanchye. After his death, before 1579, she again "consoled herself" with Robert Crispe, to whom her obliging mother leased Little Birch Hall and its estate, Crispe gaining possession in 1589. Joan, the other daughter, married Robert Spring. This wa

The Manor and the Hall

the Robert Spring towards whom as early as 1564 various people from Belchamp St. Paul and Great Yeldham were bound over to keep the peace. The disturbance must in some way have been connected with the long dispute about the Little Birch inheritance, and which for unknown reasons also involved the local Barrington family for thirty years. In 1564 Robert Waldegrave sold his moiety to Henry Golding, resident at Little Birch Hall; in 1570 Robert Spring sold his to John Bacon, who six years later conveyed it in his turn to Henry Golding, who thus became possessed of the whole. Only a few weeks later Henry Golding died and was succeeded by his brother Arthur.

The Goldings were a well-known family who had their main residence at Belchamp St. Paul. Henry Golding, who married Alice Forster, the widow of George, as her second husband, gained her life interest in half of the estate by this marriage. Although this still left him heavily in debt, he nevertheless cut a considerable figure in the county, in 1571 even becoming MP for Colchester. He extended Birch Hall at about the same time, but he must have realised as he made his will in 1575 that his efforts to create a consolidated and unencumbered estate were coming to fruition too late for him to enjoy them. His wife had not helped; Alice was a disputatious character and is known to have pushed the interests of her children by her previous marriage. Henry's will reflects this, endeavouring to secure family peace through severe penalties if the allocations of his property made by his will were contested or set aside. Easthorpe itself, however, was not in dispute and the further arguments of the Golding descendants need not detain us here.

Arthur Golding, translator and scholar, seems to have continued to live at Birch Hall off and on until 1598, despite the problem of Robert Crispe, but he was beset by even worse financial difficulties than his brother. It was no doubt for this reason that he sold Easthorpe Manor in 1577, almost immediately after his inheritance, to Richard Atkins. The arrangement to sell, at least, was made at that date but although Golding thereupon received a loan from Atkins the transaction does not seem to have been actually completed until 1583. This is no doubt due to Golding's reluctance to break up a compact holding.

There were major extensions and alterations to the fabric of Easthorpe Hall which appear to date from Atkins' time, but the Kingsmills, who succeeded, seem more likely to have been prepared to incur the expenditure; as there is some indication that these changes were carried out in two phases, it may even be that both were responsible. It is possible that Atkins was resident in 1579, in which year he presented Stephen Beaumont and is described as of Easthorpe Hall, but this could equally well mean only that he had the advowson by virtue of his ownership of the manor. There seems to be no other record, so as with his predecessors it is more likely that he was non-resident. It is, nevertheless, from about this time that the occupiers of the Hall can at last be traced with more certainty. The first of whom we have definite knowledge is Thomas Lawrence who was churchwarden in 1596.

The first mention of Thomas Lawrence is an unusual one, consisting of a long entry in the parish register which is in fact a unique insertion. From this memorandum, in the rector's hand, we learn that a certain Michael Hills came from France into England and "came to the house of Thomas Lawrence where he died of the bloody flux". James Hills, also living at the Hall, caught and died of it, as did Zachary Bays and Richard Reves, both sons-in-law of Lawrence. The rector notes that the last three of these were "purged and lay not long of the disease", which was presumably some form of plague. He also notes that five others were infected at the same time but recovered.

It nearly became a major outbreak. At Crosse House, now Well Cottage, John Amerie and two of his children are recorded as dying from the same cause within the next few weeks. Also "Mercy Richard, a poor widow, lay long after going into one Curry his house, which was infected of the bloody flux, and sickened of the same disease and died". The last of the deaths was in mid-February, and it may have been the winter season which prevented worse mischief.

In 1598 Thomas Lawrence married a certain Mary — it must have been his second marriage — and a daughter Mary was born to them the following year. In 1602, Thomas, together with Lawrence Maryon, yeoman, was bound over to keep the peace toward Thomas Stonnard of Kelvedon. Whether this Stonnard had any connection with the Stonnards mentioned in the history of Winnings is not clear; there are other occurrences of the name in the district. Several other references to this Thomas Lawrence are to be found, and from them he seems to have been living as a very minor country gentleman or moderately wealthy yeoman. A typical reference, for example, is his signing a recognisance for Richard Stokes of Lawford in 1613.

Thomas Lawrence was from a prominent family of Coggeshall clothiers. He had the temporalities of Marks Tey, and in his will of 1614 he left the parsonage there to his sons: John Lawrence was resident at the time. His lease of Easthorpe Hall he likewise left to his sons, but provided that his wife Mary should "have the parlour for her dwelling with right of egress and regress". Perhaps his sons did not take to their stepmother. The burial of Widow Lawrence is recorded in 1623.

The Lawrences' lease was from the Kingsmills. George Kingsmill, who came from a Hampshire family and was knighted in 1603, had purchased the manor from Richard Atkins in 1593. He also held Bourchiers Hall in Messing, which would certainly have been considered the more important of the two. On his death he was succeeded by his son, Sir William.

The occupancy of Easthorpe Hall remained meanwhile with Nathaniel Lawrence, who died in 1635. He describes himself in his will as "yeoman", and although six silver spoons are mentioned there is no other particular sign of prosperity. Nathaniel's various children had been baptised over the years in the parish church: Elizabeth in 1622, Anna in 1623, Sarah in 1627, Aquilla in 1629, and at last a son, Nathaniel, in 1632. Nathaniel's wife, Elizabeth Anna, may quite possibly have been the sister of William Clarke of Fouchers (Easthorpe Green), who married Mary Lawrence in 1619.

After Nathaniel's death the family appear to have continued to live at the Hall for a while, presumably for the duration of the lease. Sarah was buried in 1637, and although by 1642 entries in the parish register had become erratic as the Civil War took its effect, the marriage of Elizabeth Lawrence to Richard Emerson is prominently recorded for that year. One puzzling record occurs as late as 1654: Commonwealth records for Easthorpe are scarce but a deed survives whereby in that year William March of Great Birch sold for the considerable sum of £145 various lands near Bockingham Hall to Nathaniel Lawrence of Easthorpe. This obviously suggests that even at this late date the Lawrences were still in residence at the Hall or elsewhere in the parish, but Nathaniel was "of Great Birch" in 1679, soon after which he died. Mary Rand, a later resident of the Hall, was a witness to the deed of 1679.

The Manor and the Hall

Before 1654 it would appear that George Kingsmill, third son of Sir William, lived at the Hall himself. There is, at least, a completely isolated and thus remarkable entry in the register for 1648, where the birth of his daughter Anne is recorded. There is also a burial slab in the church to his daughter Margaret, who died in 1652. In the chancel too is an undated stone to Anna Kingsmill, wife of George, who is stated to have survived her husband twenty four years. She may have been resident at the Hall in 1662, when she held a manor court, but a little later the family of Rand were certainly tenants. During their residence Anna may have gone to live on property her husband had held in Yorkshire, but in her later years she returned to reside at the Hall. Morant dates her death to the 1670's, but in fact it occurred in 1681, although the exact date is not recorded in the registers, since the feckless Obadiah Paul had by this time ceased to keep them. The lack of an entry is perhaps all the more remarkable because in 1675 Obadiah had married her daughter Anne; there was a son, George, by the time of Anna's death, and no doubt she had returned to the Hall to be near them.

In 1653 John Phillips, of Little Birch Holt, married Elizabeth, daughter of Richard Rand, and there is other evidence that at this date the Rands not only lived in the village but inhabited the Hall — in which case Anna Kingsmill, as well as the Lawrences, must have already been living elsewhere. Among the records of the time there is yet one further complication. In 1657 there is a record of Edward Blagrave, of Easthorpe, Gent, in connection with a deed relating to Craxes in Birch. It is an isolated reference, but no 'Gent' in Easthorpe is ever recorded as having lived anywhere but at the Hall, and there are indications of a family connection between the Blagraves and the Kingsmills.

However this may be, we do know that there were two Richard Rands, father and son, of which the elder was a well-to-do farmer with property elsewhere in the county and his origins in Ashdon, while the younger was a well-known puritan. Both witnessed the will of John Shave in 1657. The younger Richard Rand took his degree at Sidney Sussex in 1647-8, and is found as an intruder at Marks Tey soon after 1650, being ejected in 1662. As early as 1646 a certain John White was referred to the Assembly of Divines for the Easthorpe vacancy (after the expulsion of the existing rector, Thomas Johnson), and there is a manuscript addition to this list naming M. Rand. This probably means 'Mr. Rand' and is the same Richard, particularly as it is elsewhere recorded that "very few know Mr. Rand's Christian name". Whether this remarkable ignorance was in some way linked to his "exceptional sweetness of temper" is open to question. Later in life he took out a preaching licence at Boxted in 1672 and died at Little Baddow in 1692.

Although this younger Richard was named as executor of his father's will in 1670 he received no bequests. The will gives some indication of the style of life at the Hall at the time, though when the actual burial occurs in the following year the elder Richard is described as "of Fordham". Among his bequests are "my great drawing table, four joint stools, one great chest, my best featherbed, one feather bolster, my best bedstead, one copper, one pillow, one pillowbeer, one brass pot and pot hooks", all to Thomas; to Joseph "a posted bed, one featherbed and a feather bolster, a bird-eyed covering, one straw bed, a feather pillow and a pillowbeer. Also my best brass kettle, a pott kettle, also one stockpott, a potthook, and a chest my writings lie in". Other bequests include a linen cupboard, "all the rest of the the brass, one little kettle and three pewter dishes of the middle sort".

The Manor and the Hall

After the death of Anna Kingsmill the manor passed, presumably by purchase, to Thomas Green. In her will of 1679 Anna had left some copyhold lands in Little Bentley to her daughter Anne and Obadiah Paul, her son-in-law, but Easthorpe Hall and all her other various possessions were divided in the ratio two parts to her son George and one to Anne alone. Obadiah was probably already showing signs of some recklessness in property dealing and this may have been the best Anna could do to try to stay his hand. Her efforts did not succeed as her unsatisfactory partitioning of the property seems to have been speedily rearranged by the parties concerned; the Hall certainly passed into Thomas Green's hands very quickly after her death.

Green or Greene is a very common name in Essex and the interconnection, if any, between the various families is difficult to determine. Easthorpe's Thomas Green owned property in St. Osyth, but his father was from Shelley, where the old church (demolished in 1800) had several monuments bearing the arms of the Greens, three bucks trippant, no doubt in the same style as on the slab in the chancel of Easthorpe church today. Shelley Hall is supposed to have been built by a John Green who purchased the property about ten years before his death in 1595. In 1634 a visitation of the College of Heralds shows that a later John Green of Shelley, son of Robert Green of Navestock Hall, had six children already by this date, yet our Thomas Green was not born till 1645.

Thomas married Ann Eldred, of the well-known Colchester family, and so married well. Eldreds lived at Birch Hall, then Olivers, and at this date also owned Little Birch Holt, residence of the Phillips family (see Flispes). Easthorpe Hall must therefore have seemed an appropriate purchase as a place to live. The seventeenth century extensions, together with various changes to the Hall's internal arrangements, are likely to have been undertaken at this time. Several seventeenth century doors still survive.

In 1634 the Eldreds had received a coat of arms and so could style themselves gentlemen. The distinct rise in tone of Easthorpe Hall, with its resident Lord of the Manor, is best appreciated from Green's will, dated 1697, which shows a remarkable contrast with that of Richard Rand thirty years previously. Green leaves to his wife "one necklace of pearl, one gold watch, the silver tankard, the large silver cup and the cover and the silver plate which have the arms of the Eldreds engraved upon them, the two silver tumblers and the six silver spoons marked AE, the long damask tablecloth marked TG . . . and to his daughter Mary, one silver dice marked LMS, one silver porringer, two small silver cups, one silver bib-bottle, one silver whistle, one silver chain, one child's white silk mantle, all her own mothers childbed linen, one necklace of pearl containing 268 pearls . . ."

Thomas Green died the following year, but the burial of his widow, Mrs. Ann Green, did not occur till 1719. Whether she resided at the Hall all this time is uncertain but not very likely. Mary Green married Thomas Cook of Portslade, Sussex, at Easthorpe Church in 1709, and possibly her mother then moved elsewhere for a while. At all events, there is some circumstantial evidence that for a few years the Hall was occupied by a certain Daniel Hallbread, who may or may not have been a relation of the Thomas Hollowbread residing at Hellens Farm, Birch, at about the same time. Over four years there are successive entries in the deaths section of the parish register as follows: 1710, Abraham Bolsham, manservant to Daniel Hallbread; 1712, Susanna Glasscock, a friend of Daniel Hallbread; 1713, Sarah, wife of Daniel Hallbread; 1714, Daniel Hallbread.

The Manor and the Hall

There is one interesting later reference to Mary Cook. Hezekiah Haynes, of Copford Hall, had mortgaged Nevards (now Hill Farm) as security for part of his daughter's dowry on her marriage to John Cox of Coggeshall. In 1701 Cox assigned this mortgage to Mary Green. It may be that she later caused some difficulty about it, because an undated letter to Haynes from Essex Street, in London, presumably from a messenger, reports the delivery of some rings and a necklace to Mrs. Cook, "but they will not answer" (i.e. meet the purpose).

The first Thomas Green's son and heir, another Thomas, was a London attorney or sergeant-at-law. That he retained an interest for some time at least in his Easthorpe property is evidenced by a deed of 1708 relating to the boundary between the field opposite the Hall (for many years after known as Orchard Field) and Cow Meadow, then glebe land and now the garden and meadow of Well Cottage. Thomas had newly planted an orchard, but the fence between the two fields was decayed, so cattle were breaking through and damaging the young trees. Furthermore, the boundary was uneven and irregular. The arrangement was to straighten the boundary by exchanges of tiny pieces of land and for Thomas Green to mend and straighten the fence itself at his expense.

Few other details of this time survive, perhaps because Thomas lost interest in the absence of any son to inherit. He died in 1726. His next heir is said by Morant, echoed elsewhere, to have been "incapable at law of inheriting", which may have meant that he was feeble-minded. Who this 'next heir' was is not clear, but the estate consequently descended through co-heiresses, one of whom, Elizabeth Blandford of Stockwell in Surrey, was married to a certain George Baker. George is said in the papers of Nathaniel Hillyer, a later owner, to have been born at his father's premises on Fish Street Hill about 1681, to have married Elizabeth in 1705, to have been a member of the Goldsmiths Company, and to have been a haberdasher and hatter in that same family house on Fish Street Hill. The relationship with Green appears to have been through his Eldred mother.

Among the children of George and Elizabeth Baker were John, who married Maria Applebee (aunt of John Applebee, rector 1796-1826), and Elizabeth, who married Nathaniel Hillyer the elder, to whom on failure of the other lines the property eventually came. Nathaniel married Elizabeth Baker in 1732 at St. Paul's. Their son was another Nathaniel who in his turn inherited in 1783 on the death of his father. This son married Susannah Sharrer at Sherborne Abbey in 1780, thereafter living for the most part fashionably at Bath. At his death in 1810 the Hall and Manor passed to his younger daughter, Susannah, who was an artist of some skill, and who married the Hon. Thomas Cranley Onslow. After that the history of the property is its descent through the same family, that of the Onslows of Clandon Park in Surrey, until sold to the Sherwoods early in this century. It is notable that although the Onslows did not reside, the woods and coverts were not leased with the Hall but were retained in their own hand, no doubt for sporting purposes. Their name is remembered in the Onslow Cottages which stand in the village at this day.

Throughout all this time the Hall was known as Hall Farm, a steep and sudden descent indeed after its rise to elegant glory under the Greens. No Baker or Hillyer ever lived there, and so its fabric was little changed. For many years the occupants were the family of Osborne, whose tombs can still be seen at the west side of the church porch,

The Manor and the Hall

conveniently visible across the moat of the Hall. A certain Thomas Osborne seems to have been the first, but he was soon succeeded by a John. The will of this first John Osborne, who died in 1746, is a throwback to that of Richard Rand, beyond the Greens: the furniture of the hall chamber goes to his wife, and that of the parlour to his unmarried daughter. His son, another John, thereafter farmed the land for nearly forty years until his own death. This is a long period in village life, and though little appears in the records to illuminate it, John Osborne's tenancy of the large farm at the centre of the village must have seemed a permanency to the inhabitants of the time. No doubt it startled the entire village when the second John Osborne remarried in old age, and the story of this is recounted under the No Name in Chapter Six. That the Osbornes were prosperous amongst their kind is evident from the land which this second John left in Mount Bures and Wormingford, and indeed he had set up his own son, yet another John, as a farmer at Great Wigborough. In his will he thought it best not to disturb this arrangement, so directed that all should be sold up and his son receive the proceeds. Despite this bequest it appears that John Osborne the third did continue farming Hall Farm himself for a few years, and indeed he was eventually buried at Easthorpe in 1807. His tomb survives.

The Osborne Tombs

At some time just before the end of the eighteenth century Hall Farm was taken on by William Potter. This was not William Potter of Winterfloods, who died in 1821, but another of the same name. Hall Farm William Potter's wife was Elizabeth, and he owned the blacksmith's shop at Great Birch, occupied by a William Hutley — no doubt the same William Hutley who bought Hoggets and was involved in a number of minor land deals around this time. By William Potter's will of 1824 he directed that the farm was to be sold up at the expiry of the lease, and this does seem to have been done by his son, another William. The tombs of both the first William Potter of Hall Farm and of William Potter of Winterfloods are still visible in the churchyard.

The Manor and the Hall

The next tenant was Daniel Smith, who farmed there for half a century until his death in 1871 at the age of 88, and then his son, another Daniel, after him. He had two wives, both of whose tombs may be seen with his own in the churchyard, not far from the Potters. He was born at Great Bardfield, and the progress of his life at the Hall may be traced to some extent through the census returns. In 1841 the farm must have been quite a lively place with Daniel and his wife, his son of 28 and his daughter Susannah; they had two servants in their twenties, one with two small children, and another little servant girl aged ten. Ten years later only Daniel with a new wife and one servant of seventeen years old were in residence, and though by 1861 his niece had joined them it must have seemed empty by comparison with earlier years.

When the younger Daniel gave up the lease, shortly before his death in 1891, the Hall ceased to be a farmhouse. The elaborate tombstone to Thomas Steed Doe of Easthorpe Hall, who died in 1909, may be seen in the churchyard. The next owners were the Sherwood family, and they were for some time resident themselves. Until recently the Hall, still a highly desirable and distinguished house in which to live, was once again leased out, much as it used to be through so many earlier centuries, but it is now occupied by Mr. Nat Sherwood.

Chapter Three
THE CHURCH AND RECTORY

Some observations about clues to the origins of the church and its parish boundaries have already been made in the first chapter. There is other evidence, albeit hard to interpret, in its dedication to St. Mary the Virgin. Little Birch and Great Birch have the same dedication, as do the nearby churches of Kelvedon, Layer Marney, Layer Breton (probably), Layer de la Haye (possibly), Peldon, Virley, Salcott and Langenhoe. For some distance further afield this dedication becomes conspicuously less common.

Easthorpe Church

The oldest architecture of several of these churches likewise has interesting parallels. Many of them are, or are known to have been, small Norman churches of similar pattern to Easthorpe. In the case of Easthorpe itself, its architectural likenesses to the ruined church at Little Birch are quite marked, and from the few illustrations that exist of Great Birch Church prior to its rebuilding in 1850 it is reasonable to suppose that it too was not dissimilar.

This is not the place for a detailed architectural description of the Church itself which is basically twelfth century with a thirteenth century chancel and lancet windows, several fourteenth century windows, and a rebuilt fifteenth century porch: full account may be seen in the RCHM Lists. A number of features are mysterious however, or have disappeared, and some of these are of unusual interest. Holman's eighteenth century manuscript notes contain a number of illuminating details.

The Church and Rectory

One notable loss since Holman's time has been the glass in the chancel windows. In the east window there was glass believed to be "exceedingly ancient" and showing the arms of the Gernons, who may well have been responsible for the replacement of the apse by the present chancel. Perhaps the glass was faded or damaged, because other visitors thought the arms to be those of the Baynards: Richard Baynard of Messing married Grace, widow of John Peyton, in 1417. Other arms were in the south window near the pulpit. In the north window, according to Holman, was a picture of an armed man with a red cross on his breast, his helm taken off by one angel and lifted up under each arm by other angels. All this glass would have been interesting to see in relation to the surprisingly large stone heads which still exist at the edges of the lancets. Holman also mentions coats of arms in three of the four sections of the quatrefoil window in the lowside arch: the top one was of the Gernons, the two middle ones held those of Spicer (see history of Spicers) and Guildsborough (see history of the Great Guildhouse), while the fourth set seems already to have been missing. The original purpose of this lowside arch, which does not seem entirely suitable for a tomb, is uncertain.

The church also once had less sightly features. A vestry was built on its north side in about 1850, and a doorway cut through to it, but it was subsequently demolished. Against this vestry stood a huge brick buttress believed to have been erected in about 1790, but this too was later demolished; the fifteenth century window which once lit the roodloft was discovered at the same time. Prior to the restoration of 1915 the exterior walls were lath and plastered, a feature also dating from the work of 1850.

The now very faint wallpaintings presumably were much more extensive at one time, but there is no record of this. Those which survive are thought to date from about 1300. The most visible are those showing our Lord with his hands uplifted in blessing, and another nearby picture (on the left-hand jamb) of an angel supporting a cross, with faint outlines of another below. On the right-hand jamb there is a figure of a winged angel, possibly supporting the emblems of the passion. The other figures still just visible are those of another angel and an ecclesiastic.

A few objects, apparently known before the 1910-1915 restoration, have now disappeared, thought to have been removed by the rector of the time and used in a rockery. These include fragments of a stone coffin, and portions of its lid with a foliated cross, probably thirteenth century. Much stranger than these is the stone which the RCHM says was formerly built into the wall above the south doorway, "with an erotic carving of a woman and the inscription ELUI: twelfth century or earlier, condition good". This stone, at that time in the rectory garden, was some time later removed to the Castle Museum in Colchester, where it may still be seen. Easthorpe church was no Kilpeck or Barfreston, and the style of this stone is quite clearly foreign to it in every respect. Even the type of stone is rare in the district, and where it can have come from is entirely mysterious.

There are a number of accounts of the restoration of the church, and several photographs of it without its roof. This restoration does seem to have been a necessary one, as there are reports of the church having been for some years neither wind nor weather proof. The roof which was so totally replaced was of no particular note, and on the credit side the discoveries which were made on the stripping of the previously stuccoed walls are interesting and valuable. Neither the niches nor the apsidal end were previously known from structural evidence, and all five of the Norman windows

The Church and Rectory

were blocked. It should not be forgotten that the present appearance of the church, therefore, which is striking in respect of its number of windows and their relative positioning, is wholly recent and was never intended at any time by any of its builders.

The rectory, which has been known in recent years by such inappropriate names as 'grange' or even 'priory', remains an interesting building but is much changed both inside and out. It stands away from the other buildings of the village and faces the largest portion of its original glebe. The rectory is very large, and clearly has been so at least from the late sixteenth century; why this should be, in such a small and not especially well-endowed parish, is not easy to explain. Gamaliel Beaumont, writing in the 1637 terrier, seems to have thought the same when he described the house as "an ancient parsonage house and parlour, hall and other rooms, with barns, stable and other edifices sufficient for so small a living". The original house was the west range, which dates from the early fifteenth century. It was extended later in the same century, but the main house, disregarding various later additions, is of about 1600. Many of the windows are of similar date but in most cases they have been extensively restored; others are nineteenth century replacements. Frequent alterations and replacements of detail, dating from the nineteenth century onwards, give the house a somewhat confusing appearance architecturally.

The 1637 terrier goes on to describe the glebe. A field of five acres abuts northward upon the "playing place", which presumably served Easthorpe as a sort of village green since space did not exist in the centre of the village itself. These five acres contained the rector's orchard and were not a single field but a number of enclosures now incorporated into the rectory grounds. The "ancient chaseway" he recorded to its east is of unknown origin and apparently caused the rector himself some puzzlement. On the other side of the road from the house there were fourteen acres in two fields, and "the hithermost to the house of the two hath at the further end southward a parcel of land separated by a quick hedge for a pasture containing one acre and three poles". The other field had a similar close. A semi-circular footpath, leaving then rejoining the road, today still follows the boundary of the two fields. They were a little separated from Portfield or Porchfield (lying east of Great Guildhouse or 'Cooks Croft') which too was glebe, but together they made a compact holding.

The rector also had Well Close, by which was meant the long field behind the present day Well Cottage. The position of this field gives cause to suspect that Well Cottage may have had some early ecclesiastical origin, but there is no evidence to confirm it. The only other glebeland is the land surrounding the church itself on two sides, and on the street end of which the schoolhouse was later built. Beaumont does not refer to this, presumably because he considered it part of the church curtilage.

In the same terrier the rector has a number of interesting references in his description of tithable land. Of Little Birch Holt he says "the ancient way for the tithes of the same lying out of Easthorpe Street between the house of the smith lying in Little Birch and the house where Shave dwelleth". That is a clear and correct description of the Birch boundary and the present footpath. He mentions at the edge of Fann Wood "a parcell of land which anciently hath been known fenced but now lyeth open to the chaseway leading to Messing Hall . . ."; this was tithable, and was not to be forgotten he says. There is also, as mentioned earlier, a reference to "the lands of the town" having a tenement called Dodwells with yards and lands near upon twenty acres".

The Church and Rectory

Of the early rectors of the parish little of interest can be said. Some can be identified with a degree of probability, but they remain hardly more than a series of names. Almost all the known names are in Newcourt's Repertorium, the usual source, and the most notable discovery since has been that of a much earlier reference than any known to him, namely one Nicholas, rector in 1214. This Nicholas, however, was clerk to the Bishop of Ostia, and this was one of the 'scandalous presentations' of English livings to foreigners by King John, into whose hands the manor and gift had temporarily fallen. Nicholas also had Great Birch, but it is most unlikely that either parish ever saw him. Nicholas, of course, was not Easthorpe's only pluralist rector, nor was he the only non-resident. Even so, aristocratic names are not common; the only two obvious examples occur early and are those of Roger Gernon and Oliver Oliver. The latter exchanged in 1367 with Robert Dyn of Aylesford, and Robert was soon embroiled in a major dispute with Leighs Priory, founded by the Gernons and in Robert's day still with local connections, including the presentation of Great Birch. Unfortunately neither the details of the dispute nor the final result are known, although Robert Dyn was still rector of Easthorpe in 1374.

Nothing is known of the lengthy tenure of the living by Simon Baron, 1408-39, but the successor after his death was a man of some eminence, the only man of national importance to have been rector. This was William Gray, at an early stage of his illustrious career, but already prebendary of Kentish Town and a canon of St. Pauls. He held the living seven years, accumulating several others during the same period, but it is doubtful whether he ever came to the parish. He went on to become a notable and prolific scholar of his day, and Bishop of Ely.

Gray exchanged in 1446 with Thomas Segg. Segg held the living of Great Bentley from 1424-1440, then resigning in favour of Feering. Unlike Gray it appears he was not a pluralist and is more likely to have been resident, farming his glebe. He did not resign Easthorpe until 1470, when he must have been at an advanced age.

The next two rectors were involved in a curious exchange. John Lester, or Lyster, was vicar of Great Birch 1474-84, in which year he resigned. Nicholas Palmer, rector of Easthorpe since 1470, thereupon became vicar of Birch as well — the last, in fact, before the line of rectors begins in 1505. In 1487, however, Lester apparently wished to get back to the district, as he exchanged another living with Palmer to become rector of Easthorpe. In the lists of incumbents their positions thus appear as the exact reverse of what they had earlier been. Lester died in 1493.

Robert Finney or Finnay, who was presented at Lester's death in 1493 was of Kings Hall, Cambridge, where he was a scholar and fellow from 1494 to 1509. After his resignation in 1495 he is not known to have held any living elsewhere. His successor is mysterious: a William Taylor or Tyler was admitted to Kings in 1493 as 'a scholar from Eton', but it hardly seems possible that it can be he who succeeded in 1495.

The first rector of whom anything of local interest is known — indeed, it could be said he was Easthorpe's only really interesting rector — is John Kingston, 1528-58. From 1530 he was also rector of Great Birch, and from 1555 of Aldham as well, but he always lived at Easthorpe. His survival unscathed through the various religious changes of his time is remarkable, because his Roman Catholic sympathies must always have been clear. As a parish priest he seems to have been conscientious. Many of the wills surviving from his time were jotted down at bedsides or were subsequent

The Church and Rectory

memoranda of oral statements; it is less surprising that there are none such before his time than that they ceased so abruptly with his death. None at all occurs during the time of his successor, Thomas Foster. Many of the wills to which Kingston was witness give an impression of care in drafting, or of a prompting of the dying testator to think of everything he should. This impression is strengthened by a comparison with the much more peremptory style of the two Beaumonts when some years later they — equally conscientious — attempted the same thing.

During the reign of Queen Mary, Kingston quite suddenly sprang to public prominence. It is likely that he was picked out as a reliable man by the famous Bishop Bonner on one of his reputedly frequent visits to his residence at Copford. Kingston was appointed Commissary, or agent, of the Bishop, and as such he had the unenviable task of conveying religious prisoners, many subsequently martyrs, from Colchester to London. Kingston took great pains to do his duty, and it distressed him that he had to deal with so hostile a population. There are interesting accounts of the problems he faced in Foxe's Book of Martyrs, where Foxe quotes a long letter from Kingston to Bishop Bonner in August 1557.

Kingston complains in this letter that he had been led to believe that he would have time to prepare for the difficult task of transporting twenty two heretics to London, but then "Mr. (Antony) Brown commanded me this afternoon, being 30th August, to go and receive my prisoners by and by. And then I said, it is an unreasonable commandment, for that I have attended on you here these three days, and this Sunday early I have sent home my men. Wherefore, I desire you to have a convenient time appointed, wherein I may know whether it will please my lord, my master, to send his commissioners hither, or that I shall make carriage of them unto his lordship. Then Mr. Brown said, we are certified that the council have written to your master to make speed, and to rid these prisoners out of hand; therefore go and receive your prisoners in haste. I answered, Sir, I shall receive them within these ten days. Then Mr. Brown said, the limitation lieth in us, and not in you, therefore get you hence.

"I replied, Sir, you have indicted and delivered me by this indenture, whose faith and opinions I knew not, trusting you will grant me a time to examine them, lest I should punish the Catholics. Well, said Mr. Brown, for that cause ye shall have time between this and Wednesday. And I say unto you, Mr. Bailiffs, if he do not receive them at your present hands on Wednesday, open your doors and let them go.

"Then said I, my lord, and masters all, I promise to discharge the town and county of these heretics within these ten days. The lord Darcy answered, commissary, we do and must all agree in one, wherefore do ye receive them on or before Wednesday.

"To which I replied, my lord, the last I carried, I was going betwixt the castle and St Catherine's chapel two hours and a half, and in great press and danger, wherefore this may be to desire your lordship to give commandment to Mr. Sayer being bailiff here present, to aid me through his liberties, not only with men and weapons, but that the town clerk may be ready there with his book to write the names of the most busy persons, and this upon three hours warning: all which both my lord and Mr. Brown commanded".

Kingston had other worries too. A married priest was in gaol with his wife, giving his name as Pullen, but Kingston was sure he was Robert Smith, canon of Appledore. Then again, various standing hospitals in and around Colchester had not appeared at

30

The Church and Rectory

any visitation. On pastoral matters, Kingston considered that "if the householder might be compelled to bring every man his own wife to her own seat in the church in time of divine service, it would profit much."

The inventory of the church goods made for the Commissioners of Edward VI in 1552 is remarkable not only for its exceptional length and obvious accuracy and completeness, but also for its evidences of the character of Kingston himself. It is interesting to see that the long list of "goods present in the church" exhibits quantity rather than quality; the values are written against each, though for some reason subsequently crossed out, and in most cases are only a few pence. Pask, pyx, chrysmatory and candlesticks are all of latten, not silver, and the "cruyts" are of tin. There are corporas cases, banner staves, several hutches (one "called the poor man's box") and a "cake of wax waying X pd.". There is also a sepulchre, presumably of the portable kind. There are even "six torches with a coffin to stand in". That obits had only lately been discontinued is implied by the large amount of money being held for that purpose. There were several bells: "two handbells with knerpulls", a "sanctus bell with wyer for the string", and a "sacrye bell". The church also appears to have had as many as three bells in its tower, two of which had been sold leaving their "gongons of brass" behind. As to vestments, a few remained but most had already been sold to "Gilbert a joyner then dwelling in St. John's parish in Colchester".

Kingston made his will a few months before his death in 1557 and, as mentioned in the history of his house called Winnings, makes it abundantly clear that he feared the Catholic cause was doomed, and that after Mary's death the laws would change; in some ways he was indeed dying at the right time. He also makes it plain just how much effort needed to be put into ensuring that local churches had at least the essential vessels for divine service after so many having been confiscated or purloined under the two previous reigns. He bequeaths "to the parish church of Easthorpe a cross copper and gilte with a fonte of the largest sort"; to Much Birch "such ornaments as are wanting for the service of divine celebration to the value of ten shillings", to Aldham a similar sum for "ornaments lacking about the altar"; to Little Tey "a small altar which I lent to Much Birch to the hands of Barton he being churchwarden and other bowles and ornaments for divine ministration".

Kingston's benefactions to the poor were generous, and to his friend the parson of Copford he left his "great gelding". The impression his lengthy will gives is of a piece with the rest of his surviving writing, that of a painstaking man striving carefully to do right. His concern for his own soul was expressed as follows: "To my brother priests dwelling within Witham, Colchester, Tendring and elsewhere willing to say a dirge and mass for the soul of John Kingston and all Christian men in their own churches four pennies each. To John Comands in London to the intent that he will vouchsafe to say St. Gregory's trentall for one John Kingston and for all Christian souls eleven shillings".

This conscientious parish priest was buried in the chancel of Easthorpe Church and presumably still lies there. He well deserves to be remembered. His heavy duties and responsibilities in the 1550s do not appear to be reflected in any diminution of concern for his home parish of Easthorpe. The contrast with the succeeding rector, Thomas Foster, is striking, and there must have been many in the parish who missed him.

Foster is an obscure figure. He is usually identified with the Thomas Foster who matriculated at Christ's, Cambridge, in 1560 and was scholar there 1561-2, but this

The Church and Rectory

does not seem to be compatible with his presentation to Easthorpe in 1558, a date which is certain. There are at least three other Thomas Fosters recorded at the university who seem just as probable. The Easthorpe Foster arrived from West Mersea, to which he was presented in 1555 and from which he resigned in 1558. In 1562, however, he was presented to Messing, apparently resigning from that parish in 1571. At or about the same time (no exact date is known) a Thomas Foster appears at Runwell, and was dead in early 1579, just as the Thomas Foster of Easthorpe, so this is almost certainly the same man. The most probable conclusion is that Foster, if he ever resided at Easthorpe, did so only briefly during his first few years.

Foster was succeeded by the Beaumonts — Stephen, 1579-1609, and Gamaliel, 1609-41 — and although their incumbency shows evidence of a sharper, more combative parochial concern than that of Kingston, at least there is a return to obviously resident and active parish priests. The Beaumonts were protestants, perhaps extremely so; Stephen Beaumont, aided and abetted by his churchwardens, Thomas Pudney and John Cranfield, was charged in 1583 with refusing to wear the surplice or to read from the book of common prayer or to administer the Sacrament, instead "celebrating seditiously other services". So seriously was this taken and so obdurate was Stephen that a date was eventually set for his deposition, but this was apparently never enforced. Perhaps he came up with some such excuse as his colleague of Great Birch, Simon Cook, who in 1585 explained that he did not wear the surplice "because it is not to be worne, it is so old and torne."

Stephen Beaumont was born in Cambridge and educated at the King's School there before being admitted pensioner at Caius in 1572. He took his degree three years later, and three years after that he was ordained deacon at Ely. He is recorded as being ordained priest at London in 1580, the year after being presented to Easthorpe by Richard Atkins of Easthorpe Hall. He soon afterwards marked his preferment and assured income by marrying Katherine Pudney, probably a local girl, and the births of their various children are recorded in succeeding years. The second of his sons Gamaliel, was born in 1581 and in due course became the next rector. Gamaliel matriculated at St. Johns, Cambridge, in 1598, taking his BA in 1601, and his MA in 1608 becoming rector of Easthorpe almost immediately thereafter. It has been suggested that his father's resignation in his favour may have been due to extreme non conformity, but it is more likely to have been the result of failing eyesight. Stephen's handwriting deteriorated noticeably from about 1604 and later on as witness to wills he could only make a mark. His death occurred in 1616 and that of his wife two years later. Their eldest son, also Stephen, died the following year. The death of their daughter "Susan Beaumont, alias Purkiss, wife of William Purkiss" occurred in 1621 when she was 35; the curious expression of this entry in the register invites speculation as to its meaning. A few other incidents in the lives of the Beaumonts are known, and these are recorded under the house histories where appropriate.

Thomas Johnson, who succeeded Gamaliel Beaumont in 1641, may have been less respectable; certainly he was no strict puritan. It is not necessarily disgraceful to have appeared before the Committee of Plundered Ministers in 1645-6, even when accused of being "a frequenter of taverns, a tippler, often drunke, and a prophaner of the holy name of God by swearing by it", but perhaps it is a little more suspicious that he should have been summoned at Quarter Sessions "to answer such questions as the Court shall put to him concerning Anna Courland, his servant". He was one of those incumbent

The Church and Rectory

reinstated at the Restoration, and held the living till 1668, when his burial is recorded. That of his wife, Dorothy, is recorded in the following year. Johnson's origins are uncertain, but he is probably to be identified with one of three Cambridge men of that name, one matriculating at Emmanuel in 1611, another a pensioner at the same college in 1617, and the third matriculating at Christ's in 1613 but obtaining his degree at St. Catherines in 1616-17.

During Johnson's deprivation the incumbency of the parish is not entirely clear. It was, perhaps, too small and too poor to attract any very enthusiastic preacher. The probability is that John Okely (BA 1641-2, of Emmanuel College, Cambridge) held it with Feering after Johnson had lost the revenues. Okely is shown as the incumbent in a parochial inquisition of 1650 (Patron "Mr. Kingsmeale" — Kingsmill), but he was already complaining that rents of five marks a year had been detained for two and a half years, and in that same year went to Stanway. Apparently he relinquished Easthorpe at the same time, because some sort of temporary supervision was thereafter exercised by John Whiting, incumbent of Lexden from the same year. This John Whiting seems to have resided at Easthorpe from as early as 1647, in which year he found it inconvenient to get to Little Totham, at least in bad weather. He certified that the parish's maintainable stretch of the London Road had been put in repair, but other than that nothing is known of him till his unusual death in 1657. In that year "he put his finger into a man's mouth whose throat was ill of a quinsy and non compos mentis he bit it vehemently, on which it gangrened and killed him about eight days later". From this time, and quite possibly before it, care of the parish passed to Richard Rand (mentioned under the Hall) and it was he who was ejected at the Restoration.

During and even after the Commonwealth period Easthorpe became in a small way something of a Puritan centre. Three, and possibly as many as five, Puritan ministers are known to have farmed in the parish, as well as others in the area around. The puritan sympathies of some of the inhabitants are mentioned in the house history chapters, and it is noticeable how these families tended to inter-marry until they had dispersed or died out by about 1720 or so. The families of Damyon and Phillips are good examples of the kind. Families new to the district in the Commonwealth, such as the Chandlers, can also be shown to have had similar sympathies; it is as though like were seeking like. The phraseology of many wills and the choice of first names in certain families are other indications. The extent of this influence is well beyond the bounds of a single parish and hence of this book, but Easthorpe has enough evidence to show that such a study of the district could be rewarding.

After the brief incumbency of John Beal (who may or may not have been the John Beal who was chaplain to Charles II) the rector for the remainder of the seventeenth century was the extraordinary Obadiah Paul, also rector of Little Birch from 1672-94. Paul matriculated at Magdalen Hall, Oxford, in 1660 and took his BA there in 1663. His MA, however, was obtained from Trinity Hall, Cambridge, in 1670, and he signed for priest's orders in London in the same year. At about the same time he was active in Kent as deacon of Bapchild and as curate of Leysdown, Isle of Sheppey, in 1668-9. He also sought a licence for the sequestration of the rectory of Warden in the same county. In 1672 he sought a dispensation in respect of the rectory of Aythorp Roding, but this seems to have dropped when he obtained the more convenient additional benefice of Little Birch in the same year. The parish registers well illustrate the further progress of his career. For the first three or four years the entries are normal enough, and they

The Church and Rectory

show nothing remarkable until we read that Obadiah Paul was married to Ann Kingsmill by the rector of Copford. As recounted under the history of the Hall, Ann was the daughter of the Lady of the Manor, and was 27 at this time. Two sons, both called George after Anne's father and her brother, were born in 1678 and 1680, the second one surviving. Soon after this marriage Paul's handwriting becomes larger and wilder, and the entries become erratic and prone to error. Eventually they cease altogether.

Other evidence shows that after Paul married money, it went to his head. He quickly launched into a great number of land deals in and around the parish, both purchases and mortgages. One such deal was Craxes in Birch. This had actually been obtained by George Kingsmill, his brother-in-law, in 1670: Anne took it over on her marriage, but in 1681, after the death of Anne's mother, Obadiah seems to have taken its management into his own hands. It appears that he made so many purchases and other rearrangements that he outran his resources or spent his money foolishly; at all events, it is clear that he was soon obliged to begin unloading them again. 1682 seems to have been a particularly bad year, possibly because of financial arrangements after the death of his mother-in-law, but not long afterwards his affairs fell into confusion. More than one lawsuit well into the next century was occasioned by the difficulty in establishing land rights hopelessly obscured by his endless trading.

Obadiah Paul's later years seem to have been spent at least partly in Messing, his widow staying on there after his death in 1703. A 1704 entry in the Easthorpe register, by then apologetically resumed by the next rector, reads, "Edward, son of Mr. William Clarke of Tollesbury and Judith his wife, being at Mr. Paul's house in Messing parish. In 1705 it was reported that some tiles were missing from the church and the pavement needed repair in several places. Significantly too, perhaps, "there wants two locks and keys to the chest and the register book must be kept in it".

John Brasier, the next rector, was an altogether different man. Although he did have clerical ancestors his father was a Colchester ironmonger, and the future rector was born there in 1667, proceeding in due course to Felsted School. At the age of 17 he was admitted pensioner to Christ's College, Cambridge, and took his BA in 1688-9, and his MA in 1692. From his few surviving writings he comes across as rather pedestrian and it seems likely that such a contrast to Paul would have been deliberately chosen. Brasier's first living was at Great Holland where he became rector in 1692 and which he retained in plurality with Easthorpe until his death. This may have been in connection with the Greens at the Hall, who presented. The Greens owned land in Chich St. Osyth, and in due course one of Brasier's daughters married the rector there, another that of Great Clacton. Whether he resided at Easthorpe is therefore doubtful, but his wife Ann seems to have lived in the rectory till her own death in 1755, no less than thirty years after that of her husband and his burial at Trinity Church, Colchester.

Ann Brasier was no doubt allowed to reside at the rectory all this time because both the following rectors were determined absentees. William Boys, who succeeded her husband, came from a wealthy background and never resided. His family were prominent merchants (and mayors) of Colchester, but there was also a widespread clerical branch having incumbents at or around his time at Coggeshall, Messing, Aldham, Little Tey, West Bergholt and elsewhere. He himself was the son of Alderman William Boys who died in 1714, being born in 1683 and educated in Colchester, then

The Church and Rectory

matriculating at St. Johns, Cambridge in 1698. He gained his BA in 1701 and his MA in 1705. In 1706 he was presented by his father to West Bergholt, and Easthorpe came his way in 1725. He died on 20th January, 1734.

John Halls, the next rector, was the incumbent for over sixty years, and thus may be seen as to some extent typifying the slumberous state of the Church of England in the eighteenth century. During his time, while equally interminable Osbornes occupied Hall Farm, it can at least be said that the registers were maintained and the church was buttressed to prevent collapse, but it is difficult to think that the cause of religion in the small parish was otherwise much furthered by that wealthy and absentee rector, a man of latitudinarian views. The only parish record which bears his personal mark is a note of the payment of the Winnings Charity written in a neat hand.

John Halls was the son of Robert, a noted Colchester attorney, and was born in 1708. He went to school at Bury, and became a pensioner at St. Johns, Cambridge, in 1725. He matriculated in 1727 and LLB in 1731. He was rector of Easthorpe before his twenty seventh birthday, but presumably lived somewhere in Colchester, perhaps at his father's house, while Ann Brasier lived on at his rectory. In 1747 he married Elizabeth Selly, whose mother was a very wealthy Colchester brewer. Soon after his marriage Halls built or largely rebuilt the handsome house of Greyfriars, Colchester: most of what is seen today is his work. In this fashionable splendour he lived until his death, his Easthorpe glebe being farmed in later years by Thomas Firmin. He was not a pluralist, but his single small rural parish cannot have been the foremost of his concerns. At his death in 1795 he was described as a most benevolent and universally respected character.

Both the next two rectors were relations of the lords of the manor. John Baker, son of George and Elizabeth, married Maria Applebee: he died in 1796, and this was the year of John Applebee's preferment to the parish. Maria left this John, her nephew, £3000. John Hallward, rector from 1826-44, was similarly in receipt of legacies from both Nathaniel and Susannah Hillyer.

Rev. George Bowles c1860, (from old Photograph)

The Church and Rectory

With the Rev. George Bowles, rector from 1844 till his death in 1878 we enter the received memory of the village. A few stories of him are still told, and at least two photographs of him are extant, one showing him outside the rectory in his trap. An amusing story relates how he was puzzled by a gap in the rectory hedge, in fact caused by the irruption of a local youth (a Hale of Copford, a well-known local name) on his excursions to woo the parlourmaid. Bowles' unexpected problems with witchcraft are related under the history of the Flispes. His later years were sad, for he is reported never to have recovered from the death of his son, George Herbert, who was drowned in 1857 at the age of 18 whilst serving with the 85th Light Infantry. The rector's substantial tomb, with a lengthy and still decipherable but crumbling inscription, may be seen behind the church.

The census records provide an interesting glimpse of the lifestyle of the rectors of the time, and it is worth remembering when reading them that Easthorpe parish never had more than two hundred souls so cannot have been too demanding a cure. In 1838 there were "but one or two dissenters in the parish". In 1841 the man who wrote that, John Hallward, aged 52, lived at the rectory with his wife and his son John, 18. The schoolmistress, Rebecca Bradley, was also 18 and was a lodger: unfortunately the census does not relate whether this caused any difficulties! There were also five servants, being two men and three women, only one over the age of 26. In 1851 George Bowles, then 43, lived much less extravagantly; presumably, unlike Hallward, Bowles had no legacies to supplement his income. In that year the rectory housed him, his wife, five daughters and a son, but they had only three servants, all women.

One later event is worthy of remark. When the benefice was united with that of Copford, the rector of the time cursed the parish; he also had a number of other known — and still to be remembered — eccentricities. The curse is carefully preserved in the parish chest.

Chapter Four
THE BADCOCKS FARMS

Great Badcocks
Great Badcocks, normally and more correctly known simply as Badcocks, is reputed to have been anciently a manor, but no records survive of meetings of its manorial court and no nearby properties are known to have come under its jurisdiction. The site, however, has an air of importance and the house was originally moated. Parts of the present structure are late fifteenth century but most, including the hall, was rebuilt in the late sixteenth century — presumably in 1585 as this date appears on a moulded bressumer; 1585 was also the year in which the property passed to Katherine Audeley. The history of Badcocks is not easy to disentangle because it seems never to have been occupied by its owner, and both owners and occupiers changed frequently.

Badcocks

During the later middle ages Badcocks was part of the Tey estate which at one time covered most of the area of several of the neighbouring parishes. They probably held it of the Peytons, whose history is recounted under Easthorpe Hall. It is known that Badcocks was held of Richard Baynard of Messing in 1473, and as the Baynards obtained their local property through the marriage fifty years before of a Richard Baynard to Grace, heiress of the Peytons, the manor may have been held with Easthorpe for some time.

The name Badcocks is presumed to have derived from a John Badcock of Easthorpe mentioned in the Feet of Fines in 1365, or from others of his family. Other Easthorpe references to the name are very few, though the name does occur elsewhere in the county; for example, another John Badcock is mentioned as owning land near Great Dunmow in 1439. Who occupied it after the Badcocks is not known, but by the elimination of other possibilities it can be shown that in the years around 1500 the family of Twede are much the most likely. It is possible that the Twedes were

The Badcocks Farms

the immediate predecessors of John Pilgrome, who died in 1538, as the Pilgromes were certainly residents, but this cannot be proved.

If John Pilgrome farmed Badcocks, as well as just living in the house, then his successors must have given it up for a time because the will of Henry Alane, 1555, shows him anxious to keep the remainder of his lease of Badcocks as a single entity and secured to his children and family. The house and the farm appear to be treated in this will as separate units so it is possible that the Pilgromes did still reside. Similarly, Alane seems nervous about the lease in general and specifically doubtful that it will be renewed. He himself was moderately prosperous, leaving as bequests "a flock bed and two pattens of the biggest sort and two of the best pewter".

If, on the other hand, Alane did in fact reside at the house as well as farm the land then his hopes were not fulfilled, for as early as the following year the next John Pilgrome died there. Pilgrome's status was that of tenant, renting from the Teys, though he owned Chippets Farm at Copford in his own right, again with the possible implication of the separation of residence and farm. In his will he left a bullock of two years old to each of his children, and a sheep to John and Joan Wharton: these appear to have been brother and sister. The Whartons were a prominent family of the time who seem to have declined. The marriage of "John Wharton and his wife, servants to Mother Pilgrome", is recorded in 1579; a John Wharton, comfortably off, and apparently the same man, died in 1596 and his will has survived, but so has that of his sister Margaret, who died poor. "Mother Pilgrome" herself, another Joan, lived nearly as long since she did not die until 1592, and her will too has survived. It is that of a rather grand old lady, with a long string of bequests to her grandchildren and to numerous friends. Her bequest to charity took the form of four bushels of wheat to eight of the poorest people of Easthorpe.

Joan Pilgrome and her son Robert are mentioned as occupying Badcocks in the year of her death, 1592, but Robert George of West Mersea is likewise mentioned as an occupier three years earlier in 1589. Robert George can be traced and was undoubtedly non-resident; he farmed other land in Easthorpe (later remembered as George's Croft) as well as much land over the parish border in Messing. It is therefore certain that Joan was living on in the house while the land was farmed by others, and this together with the earlier probabilities makes it reasonable to state that the Pilgromes resided continuously from the 1520s.

The last of the Teys in the area, Thomas Tey, feoffed Badcocks to the wealthy Katherine Audeley of Berechurch. This Thomas Tey descended rapidly in the world, selling or renting successive parts of the family estate and eventually selling even his own manor house (at Layer de la Haye) in 1594. To be fair to him, however, his forbears had been steadily selling land as early as the 1520s and the estate may have been impossibly encumbered. At the same time the Audeleys had been moving upwards; Sir Thomas Audeley, Lord Chancellor of England, formed the Berechurch Hall estate from monastic lands after the suppression of the monasteries. Katherine, described by Morant as "a bold and turbulent woman", was his nephew's wife. From her it descended to her eldest son, Robert, and after his death to his wife, another Katherine. She did not die till 1641, aged 73, and there is an inscription to her in the Audeley Chapel at Berechurch.

The ownership of the Audeleys has left no evidence of their taking any further

The Badcocks Farms

interest in the property other than ensuring that it was occupied by well-to-do residents. All the second Katherine's property at length passed to her brothers and their descendants sold it to Thomas Wharton of Grays Inn. Partitioning of the property and various mortgages make its ownership very complicated at this period, perhaps as a result of the Civil War, but Andrew Wharton, son of Thomas, found he had sufficient title in it left to sell to a certain Thomas Johnson in 1676; this may or may not have been the son of the rector of the same name who had died in 1669. If it was, then there was a certain logic in his selling it only four years later to Obadiah Paul, the succeeding rector. Paul, however, as already mentioned in Chapter 3, was buying up much other local property and overdid it; only two years later Badcocks was sold again, this time to the Creffield family, as part of a deal involving Little Badcocks and described under the history of that house.

Who occupied Badcocks immediately after the death of Joan Pilgrome in 1592 is not clear, but there cannot have been a long gap before the residents were the family of Turner. Thomas Turner was certainly there in 1614, and various children were born to him and his wife Joan before 1625. His elder son, another Thomas, died in 1635, but the date of his own death is uncertain, although it does not seem to have been long before he was succeeded by Peter Turner, his second son — but this Peter died in 1650 aged only 31. That Badcocks was thought to be a desirable residence for a minor country landowner is again evident from Peter Turner's will. He was unquestionably a wealthy man, leaving an impressive amount of property in various parts of the county, but he did not own the house in which he lived.

Peter's wife, Hannah, continued to occupy Badcocks for a few years after his death, presumably till the expiration of the lease, and thereafter the Turners are heard of in the parish no more. Later Turners were of Feering. A certain 'Reverend Mr. Turner' is shown as owning a small piece of land at the edge of Badcocks farm in 1741, but this seems to be mere coincidence. The next lessor was Daniel Grimston, but of him nothing is known except that a child of his was buried in 1668 and that he was still there in 1672.

There seems to have been no other tenant before the Porters arrived, though they are only certainly traceable from around 1690. By this time the land was apparently once again being farmed with the house, and in the absence of evidence of any other tenant it is likely that Grimston did the same. Even so, the Porters were well-to-do. They have a long history at Messing, where the main branch of the family lived at Thrushelford from about 1500 till 1727. John Porter, the first of the family at Badcocks, was so upset that the births of his three children had not been entered in the parish register during the erratic late years of Obadiah Paul that he made a special request for them to be recorded after it was properly resumed in 1703. John Brasier, the new rector, duly wrote a memorandum to that effect. As this was not done immediately, however, it seems that Porter's request was in some way inspired by his second marriage in 1706 to Mary Fisher, widow.

John Porter the elder died in 1739 and his son, another John, in 1759. John the younger's wife Elizabeth had died in 1758. Their only son was called Thomas, and he too farmed at Badcocks and was eventually buried in Easthorpe churchyard in 1788. Whether he moved elsewhere or whether, like so many of his predecessors, he continued to reside in the house for a time while the land was farmed by others, is not

The Badcocks Farms

certain, but it is known that as farmer he was succeeded by William Osborne, and that this William died in 1764.

William Osborne was the brother of the first John Osborne of Hall Farm and he bequeathed his lease to his nephew, William May, who was living in the same house with him before his death. Perhaps this was Badcocks, and Thomas Porter had moved elsewhere. William May was married and had a family; his children were baptised at Easthorpe from 1759 onwards. John May, William's father, died in 1775 when he had farmed the nearby Fouchers for twenty years; he seems to have come from Earls Colne, where he owned land, and he had married Hannah Osborne, William's sister. John May's eldest daughter, Susannah (i.e. William May's eldest sister), was the Susannah May who married William Eley of Canfields.

There are indications that this John May held a lease of Canfields for a time, though it cannot certainly be proved. Whether he did or not, he certainly knew Winterfloods, the farm next door to it, tenanted at the time by the Potters. In his will he leaves his son John May (dead by 1794) the Earls Colne property, but pays particular attention to his "natural son Richard which I begat on the body of Mary Potter". To him he leaves "£100 to be paid to the churchwardens and overseers of the poor of Easthorpe". The interest, at the rate of no less than £4 per year, was to be paid into Mary Potter's hands, and Richard was eventually to be put out as apprentice, the money for the indentures being paid from the principal. Richard cannot have been very old, so Mary must have been an old man's fancy: the remainder of John May's property was split among his six children and grandchildren. Most of these seem to have gone to live with William at Badcocks, and Mary May, one of the six, leaves a sad little spinster's will in 1794. It should also be noted here that this John May the elder appears to have been the John "Mays" whose children are recorded in the parish register as born in the 1730s and 40s If this is so, and it can hardly be otherwise, then John May was indeed farming Canfields and must have watched the young Mary Potter playing and growing up with his own children.

William May farmed Badcocks with the assistance of these numerous relatives, and many births and deaths connected with them are recorded during this time. He held the lease until 1800, but had some years previously retired to Upminster where he rented Upminster Hall and was elected churchwarden in 1792. It is perhaps surprising that the lease immediately passed from this prolific family, but they disappear rapidly from local records. The next tenant was Henry Gusterson but he held the lease for only five years before the farm passed to Thomas Hall. The Gustersons were presumably in the area at an earlier date — though it is difficult to see where — because the parish register records the marriage of a Margaret Gusterson in 1786 and an Elizabeth Gusterson in 1797; possibly they were sub-tenants of William May.

As for the ownership during this period, it had of course continued with absentee land-owning families. The Creffields had sold it by 1740 to Samuel Shepherd of Springfield, from whom it had passed to his son, the Rev. George Shepherd. By 1780 the ownership had changed again, this time to the Rev. W. E. FitzThomas, in whose family it remained many years. Captain FitzThomas, the clergyman's son, mortgaged Badcocks for £1000 as early as 1807 and thereafter it was subject to a succession of mortgages, particularly around the middle of the nineteenth century, until it was sold to Joseph Smith. Badcocks was sold to the present owners, the Sherwood family, early in the present century.

The Badcocks Farms

Thomas Hall, succeeding Gusterson, farmed Badcocks only briefly, and it soon passed into the hands of the Marthams — first John, and on his death his sons William and John. After William's death in 1815 John the younger farmed Badcocks till the expiry of the lease, apparently in 1831 or 2. Thomas Wade was the next lessor, and the census of 1841 shows him living there as a widower with his six children aged from 25 down to 13. His tombstone is still just legible in the churchyard, and reports him as having died in 1859, aged 75. His second wife survived him some fifteen years but it was his second daughter, Mira, born in 1815, who was responsible for the farm after her father's death.

Little Badcocks formerly Hewers

Little Badcocks

Little Badcocks hides behind a discouraging nineteenth century brick facade, and even inside it substantial alterations, fifty years ago, have left little of visible interest. It does, however, have a seventeenth century frame with some earlier features. Today it is owned and inhabited by Mr. Hugh Macaulay, who also farms the land.

The earliest known name of Little Badcocks is Fennes, and it was therefore presumably the residence or at least the property of Simon atte Fenne and his son William, who are mentioned in the parish in the fourteenth century, when it was a common name in the district generally. The family of atte Fenne owned an eponymous manor in Bocking at about the same time. There is no other known owner between the Fennes and the Hewers, who were owners and occupiers in the early sixteenth century if not earlier.

The first recorded John Hewer is shown in the Lay Subsidy of 1524 as having goods valued at £40 at a time when the next highest in the parish is only £8. The local importance of both them and their dwelling is thus evident. It was rich "old John Hewer" who bought a silver pyx from Marks Tey Church in 1552. It is probable that the fine fireplace which is so conspicuously displayed in the Castle Museum and which

The Badcocks Farms

comes from this house dates from the time of one of these prosperous early Hewers. Another possibility, however, is that this fireplace was removed from the Great Guildhouse, which stood opposite and was burned down in 1738. The reason for entertaining such a possibility is that in its original position the fireplace is so tall that it appears to have been constructed for a hall open to the roof, whereas there is no obvious structural evidence of the present house being as old as this. Even so, that it was the domestic hearth of the Hewers remains the more likely and simpler explanation.

John Hewer was followed by Thomas, then another Thomas, William and finally Robert. The will of the first Thomas (d. 1572) is of interest, mentioning a number of early field names. It is notable too that this is one of the very few wills which occurs during the incumbency of Thomas Foster. It is witnessed by Henry Damyon, clerk, presumably a relation of the family named Damyon who were widespread in Marks Tey and whose main residence was Damyons just across the parish boundary (see Spicers). Another witness was Henry Harrington, "lord bayley of the manor". After this Thomas the fortunes of the Hewers seem to have declined, because parts of their earlier possessions begin to appear in other ownerships. Their only recorded acquisition is by Robert Hewer in 1610; he purchased Postell Pightle (now Kildegaard by the Roman road).

Robert Hewer sold Little Badcocks house itself, by now known as Hewers and now Fennes, to William Deeth of Great Wenham. As a separate sale he transferred to Deeth various of his fields, including a holding called Abbotts, which had a dwelling upon it at this time. The Deeth family are written as "Death" in the registers. A Thomas and Grace Death have entries during 1615-17, but Grace then died. William Death and Abigail his wife had a child buried in 1619.

The scanty history of the house once on Abbotts field is best recorded here. Coggeshall Abbey had a holding in Easthorpe as early as 1291, when it was valued at £1-18s, and since no other abbatial holding in Easthorpe is recorded at any time this is most probably the land concerned. The house was inhabited from at least as early as the late sixteenth century by the Bayse or Baysey family, who occur in local records, notably those of Great Birch, where Bayseys lived at this time in "the little house by the church". The Easthorpe line ended with the death of John Baysey in 1671, after which Francis Glasscock succeeded to the tenancy. The Bayseys are not known ever to have been prosperous, and it is clear that by the seventeenth century Abbotts was too small to be independently viable. A mortgage to John Alderman is recorded, and this was assigned to John Cordell, rector of Copford, then transferred to the rector of Easthorpe, Obadiah Paul, in 1682. Although still referred to as a separate holding at this time it was already farmed with Little Badcocks and is not distinguished separately after the end of the century.

The later Hewers did not themselves always reside, as one wealthy tenant is certainly known to have both lived in the house and farmed the land. This was Thomas Pudney, who died in 1590, a year later than his wife. He owned land at Castle Hedingham, and in his will left bequests of substantial sums of money. In this will he also mentions a remarkable number of beds, so numerous that even the large family reported in the registers both before and after his death (the last entry is in 1604) can hardly have filled them all. He leaves, miscellaneously, "two pewter platters, my standing bed in the parlour, a pair of my best sheets, a tablecloth belonging to my long

The Badcocks Farms

table in the parlour, the cupboard in the hall, the bed (my son) lieth in with the bedsteadel in the chamber by it, the bed in my chamber, a flock bed in (another) chamber, a flock bed in my chamber, a chest in my chamber, a long table and a square table in the hall, a cauldron and my brasse as it hangeth".

Thomas Pudney seems to have become embroiled in the religious difficulties of his day. As already mentioned, in 1583 he was accused as churchwarden of aiding and abetting Stephen Beaumont in his refusal to wear the surplice. In the following year John Barrington, with an ally from Little Birch, was the subject of a writ to summon a jury with a view to trying him for forcibly expelling Thomas Pudney from "one messuage, one barn, 100 acres of land and 40 acres of pasture with appurtenances". This was Little Badcocks, and it would be interesting to know just how this expulsion was effected. There were several obviously related expulsions around this date, and some accounts describe a mob of about twenty, armed with pitchforks. An earlier Barrington connection with Robert Spring suggests that the incident may have been connected with the dispute already mentioned concerning rent or fees due in respect of Little Birch Hall, a case dragging through the courts at this time. Spring believed that Arthur Golding, resident at Little Birch, owed him this money: Pudney, who held land of Golding, may well have been an innocent victim.

After Pudney the next certain occupiers were the family of Shave, first heard of in the parish when John Shave married Priscilla in 1622; Thomas Shave, then William Perry, were occupiers of at least part of the land in the 1650s and 1660s, followed by (for the lands only) Francis Chatterton and Daniel Phillibrowne. John Shave probably died at the house in 1660. His will, made in 1657, describes him as "weak in body" rather than sick and he would have been elderly by this time. He seems to have been a puritan, and his will was witnessed by Richard Rand, the puritan rector of Marks Tey whose father tenanted Easthorpe Hall. Shave makes an interesting list of property bequests, including "one half-headed bedstead standing upon the chamber over the dairy, two blankets, one double coverlet, one chaff bed" also "the greatest kettle but one, one pot, one posnett, four pewter dishes of the middle sort, three pair of canvas sheets, two holland pillowbeers, one salt cellar and one porringer, one samlet, one fruit dish, a caudle pot, one canvas table cloth, half a dozen flaxen napkins, one hutch, one chest standing upon the parlour chamber, one chest standing in the parlour chamber, one washbowl". To Sarah, his daughter, "1 brasse pot". To Priscilla, his daughter·"1 great kettle". Many of these items can be identified as being dispersed among his grandchildren by Priscilla Shave, his wife, in 1675.

Little Badcocks remained with William Deeth until his death, upon which it was purchased by Samuel Taylor. Taylor appears to have put back together the lands dispersed or separately leased by Robert Hewer; for example, fields known to have been owned by Robert Hewer appear back with the main farm described as "late in the occupation of Thomas Shave and the widow Steele". After John Shave's death the Taylors seem to have taken up residence themselves; they were a widespread family, known as clothiers of Hadleigh and Colchester. Joseph Taylor, dying in 1675, is apparently wealthy but leaves no detailed inventory; his greatest expressed anxiety is that his wife should, in his words, "educate my children to read".

In 1682 Obadiah Paul, rector of Easthorpe, lent money under part mortgage of the property, so taking an interest in land adjoining other land which he had bought from Taylor two years earlier. He may have been aiming to build up an estate around the

The Badcocks Farms

rectory. In the same year he bought from John Cordell, rector of Copford, a farm which consisted of individual fields scattered amongst the Little Badcocks holding itself. These pieces of land included Oakleas and Highfields, frequently mentioned in records of the time. Also included was "a tenement near the rectory occupied by Daniel Phillibrowne". Apparently this was the tenement described in the terrier of 1637 as "two tenements under one roof" and in 1666 as "occupied by the widow Steele and Thomas Shave . . . together with a driftway". The name of this house was Joyes and of the driftway Joyes Lane. Further details of their history appear under that name in Chapter 7.

It appears that when this transaction was taking place, Obadiah Paul was raising money, perhaps to make the purchase, by selling yet other land to Elizabeth Creffield; but Paul's deals were so fast and furious that they are difficult to unravel. They were confusing even at the time, for in this case it was decided in court a century later that the ownership had remained with the Taylor family and that no one could be held responsible for Paul's debts to the Rev. Mr. Cordell of Copford. Obadiah Paul must be given one piece of credit, however; it does seem to be due to his activities that the various scattered holdings were united into what three hundred years later still largely remains the farm of Little Badcocks.

From 1694-9 the ownership of the property was with Elizabeth Creffield, who was born a Taylor, and she left it to her sister Ann, wife of Joseph Duffield — though Great Badcocks and Joyes went to her Creffield relations. The Creffields, it should be said, were a well-known and wealthy Colchester family; the heiress married James Round, eldest son of the squire of Little Birch Hall, in 1758. Joseph Duffield farmed Garlands, in Birch. On his death, in 1727, it was another Elizabeth Creffield to whom he left both Garlands and Great Badcocks, Little Badcocks remaining with the Duffields till 1763. By this time his son Thomas Duffield of Lexden, tanner, had granted a series of mortgages on the property and the ownership had become very complicated. One of these mortgages was held by Isaac Green, who had married his daughter Mary, and who after his father-in-law's death successively bought out other rights in the property so that Little Badcocks was back in single ownership and clear of debt by the time of his own death in 1799. It was then inherited by his grandchild, Joseph Cooke.

It may have been immediately after the death of Joseph Taylor in 1675 that William Wade began his tenancy of the property; he was certainly there soon after 1680. The Wades were a moderately prosperous farming family mostly active in Great Birch, but William seems to have been a popular name amongst them and it is not entirely certain just which William Wade this one was. He was, however, certainly the elder of two successive Williams in Easthorpe, the younger William Wade no doubt being his son. The younger William's first wife was called Elizabeth, but after her death he married Lydia, widow of William Thedam of Thedams Farm which once stood opposite Shemmings. When he died he left nothing to his three children, who seem already in some way to have been well provided for, and everything to Lydia. Not long afterwards she too died, desiring "to be buried near my loving husband William Wade", and left legacies to many and various relations, notably the Chattertons of Joyes, but also to the families of Turner, Shave and Polley, to all of which she was related. She even left £5 to John Brasier, "my parish minister, for his kindness in helping me with my affairs after the decease of my late husband".

Throughout much of the rest of the eighteenth century the occupiers were the

44

The Badcocks Farms

Polley family, apparently in a more prosperous condition than their numerous farm labourer descendants a hundred years later. They did not farm the entire property; some was farmed by the Osbornes at the Hall. On the other hand, they did also tenant the maltings. A malting stood just to the west of the house, against the road, from at least as early as 1666, and it appears that the tenancy of Maltings Farm, as Hewers became known at this time, always went with the village public house. This was the Bell, now Bell Cottage, which, as already mentioned, lay in a detached portion of Little Birch even though only a hundred yards from Easthorpe Church. As late as 1821 a lease was granted to James Polley, "farmer and maltster". The public house itself, however, was apparently sub-tenanted, the actual occupant being the blacksmith. As mentioned under the history of Well Cottage, the smiths were the Oddy family for a couple of centuries and in some years they certainly resided at the Bell and no doubt kept it; nor is any other occupant known. Even after their time the link remained. Thomas Hutley was responsible for the "beershop" in 1848, for example, while James was the blacksmith in 1863; there are many similar records. The Bell was eventually delicensed in 1923, in part exchange by the brewers for a major licence at Clacton.

In 1817 the farm of Little Badcocks was sold to William Hutley, the same who had bought Hoggets in 1811. James Polley already held the lease at this time; it was a fresh lease that was granted in 1821. On the death of Hutley in 1848 the farm was inherited by George Stebbing, who farmed it himself with disastrous results. Within two years he was in debt, and successive mortgages began in 1854. His wife Ann, Hutley's daughter, seems to have done her best for him but to no avail: on one occasion George's debts were so pressing that he felt obliged to abscond, leaving behind him a special order protecting her against his creditors. He was at length declared bankrupt in 1862 and the farm was assigned to Ann. On her death in 1866 their son, George Hutley Stebbing, succeeded to the farm but he too failed in 1875. It seems to have been the same man, described as "of Wickham Bishops, cattle dealer" who went bankrupt a second time in 1879.

The name Little Badcocks is unfortunate in that it creates needless confusion. It clearly derives from the joint ownership with Badcocks itself by the Duffields/Creffields in the eighteenth century, that is before 1765. By the early nineteenth century the joint ownership had long ceased, but strangely enough it is only then that the name of Little Badcocks supersedes that of Maltings Farm, and that even though the Maltings still continued. Perhaps 'Little Badcocks' had been in local colloquial use for some time. Even so, the name Maltings Farm was still sometimes used: early census returns refer to the farm under this name and in one instance actually refer to Joyes (by then its farm cottage) as Little Badcocks, though this is clearly an error.

Chapter Five
ANCIENT FARMSTEADS

Easthorpe Green

Easthorpe Green Farm, once known as Fouchers, was until recently the residence of Mr. Nat Sherwood, the major landowner of the parish. The fabric of the house is predominantly seventeenth century but has been much altered. Its site is unusual in that the house is only a hundred yards from Flispes, which is still standing though in a dilapidated condition. Flispes was subject to a different manor.

The name Fouchers must certainly refer to the family known to be resident in the parish in 1418, when a deed was witnessed by Thomas and Robert Foucher. In 1327 a Roger Foucher was here or in Birch and a William Foucher was in Layer Marney. Others bearing the name Foucher or Fucher are known in Essex as early as the twelfth century from around the Roding valley area. Another of the local branch, William Fowcher, was described in 1425 as citizen and mercer of St. Mary Aldermanbury. A later William Fowcher, of Great Birch, was on the rent-roll of Sir Henry Marney holding a considerable amount of land in both Layer Marney and Birch till about 1500 after which the name no longer occurs in the district.

Easthorpe Green formerly Fouchers

There is no other direct record of the farm until as late as 1592, when money was paid in respect of it by John Daniel to Nicholas Walle, senior. John Daniel was of Bouchiers Hall, Messing, and is mentioned in the histories of Hazells and Canfields; earlier Fouchers ownership may have been similar to these. The records make it clear that Fouchers had in fact been sold by Daniel to Nicholas Walle before 1588, but some arrangement had been made whereby Daniel borrowed five hundred pounds from Walle, for which Fouchers formed part security. At that time Daniel appears to have been pressed for money, as he was selling other land in the area too. The father of

Ancient Farmsteads

Nicholas Walle, another Nicholas, had died in 1591 and left named lands in Great Birch amongst many other possessions. From an interesting codicil to his will made very shortly before he died, it appears that Francis Baysey, of the "little house gainst the church" in Great Birch, unexpectedly purchased his dwelling for cash (though fenced off from any land), and old Nicholas revoked his earlier bequest of it. The family of Walle lived at the spectacular house of Houchins on the Coggeshall/Feering border, so certainly did not reside at Fouchers. Who did is not known, though by elimination of other possibles from the parish records the Whartons or the Cranfields appear the most likely families.

In 1629 the next Nicholas Walle sold Fouchers to Thomas and Peter Turner, the same family mentioned under Badcocks. Peter Turner, under obligation from one of these ownerships, was presented for failing to repair the churchyard fence in 1646. Throughout the rest of the century the Turners continue to be described as occupiers, but their ownership was tenuous and doubtful, and at times almost non-existent. This is because of a stream of mortgages and assignments, notably involving William Clarke and perhaps having some connection with the Civil War. The Turners at this time farmed the land from Badcocks, while Clarke resided at the farmhouse, which he purchased from Sir Edward Bullocke. Exactly how the farm had become separated from the land is not clear, but either it was split at the time of the sale by Walle or else by the Turners: the former is the more likely.

William Clarke was quite a wealthy man, owning plenty of land and property, and it is likely that the seventeenth century rebuilding of Fouchers is his work. He chose to live at Easthorpe presumably because it was the home of his wife's family: in 1619 he had married Mary, daughter of Thomas Lawrence of Easthorpe Hall. Sir Edward Bullocke was of Loftes, Great Totham, but in the year of Clarke's death purchased Faulkbourne Hall, becoming the first of seven generations of his family to reside there. Nevertheless, either William Clarke or a namesake had some connection with Easthorpe pre-dating ownership of Fouchers farmhouse, because someone of that name was presented for failing to repair the hundred yards of the parish responsibility for "the highway", despite local pressure, as early as 1602 — though in 1611, as mentioned under Scotties, he is described as "of Feering" when convicted of a similar offence. In Clarke's defence it should be noted that the Easthorpe part of "the highway", the present-day A12, was only one short length of a notoriously poor stretch "from Domsey Brook to the tree called Cross a Hand", as it was described in 1661, for which the parishes of Feering and Marks Tey were also frequently presented.

William Clarke's will is of interest. He leaves Gosbutts in Great and Little Tey, after his wife's death, to his "kinsman" William Clarke of Pebmarsh, and Scotties (Easthorpe) to James Clarke, William's brother. His main holdings were at Braxted, but the furniture he leaves is that of his residence. He makes mention of a number of bedsteads, namely "the joyned bedstead over the parlour at Fouchers"; to John Clarke the bedstead, etc. "now in the chamber where he lodges"; to Thomas Clarke the elder not only lands in Totham but the "other bedstead" in John's room. So John Clarke, perhaps the nephew of the childless William, was lodging there. Clarkes were still in evidence at Easthorpe as late as 1682, when another William Clarke married Elizabeth Damyon, but it is not certain that he ever lived in the parish. If he did, it is less likely to have been at Fouchers than at Scotties.

By the mid 1690s the Turners appear to have recovered Fouchers from all its

Ancient Farmsteads

various encumbrances and sold it, both house and farm, to Isaac Potter. During this decade the occupiers were George and Hannah Taysgill, but their occupation was not of long duration and subsequent tenants are uncertain. In 1718 Isaac Potter died and left the farm to his son, another Isaac, of Great Coggeshall.

In 1727 the death of Stephen Potter of Fouchers is recorded. The first mention of Stephen is in the manorial rental of 1698, so it may be that after the Taysgills he lived at the farmhouse and farmed the land himself. Who occupied it after that is not known, but in 1731 Isaac Potter mortgaged it to Charles Gray of Colchester, already busy accumulating the future Round estates. Isaac died in 1736 and in 1739 Fouchers was sold to Charles Gray by his executors to pay his debts. Thereafter it remained with the Round family till purchased by the Sherwoods in the present century.

John May was tenant by 1756, but it is not certain how early his tenancy commenced. In 1769 Flispes was united with Fouchers and he farmed that also till his death in 1775. By this time the Mays were established at Badcocks, as has already been described, so the farming of Fouchers passed to Henry Powell from Donyland. In 1786 his wife Mary is recorded as having been buried at East Donyland church (since demolished) at the age of 48.

In 1791 Henry was married again, to Elizabeth Moss of Easthorpe, but his curious will of 1807 implies that it had not been a close union. His bride had also been married before, and perhaps she had learned too much worldly wisdom for Henry's taste, or perhaps Henry had become obsessed about money. In his will he leaves his widow "£138 8s 8d, being the balance of monies received by me upon or in consequence of my marriage with her, after deducting such items as I have expended for the use of herself and her family". A codicil of 1812 makes no change in this exact sum allotted to his widow, but he divided the farm equally amongst his three sons, an arrangement conspicuously avoided in 1807. In 1812 he could not sign his name but only make his mark, and he died the following summer. It was during Powell's time that the name Fouchers was changed to Easthorpe Green.

Two of the Powell sons, John and James, then farmed Fouchers for some years. James had married Elizabeth Gusterson (from Badcocks) in 1797. Their twin girls were buried in 1801. Soon after 1820 John Powell surrendered the lease and Thomas King took over. Thereafter Fouchers fell victim to the agricultural depression of the 1830s, being farmed at that time by John Hutley and Lawrence Orpen with land in Feering and elsewhere. John Hutley was of the blacksmith family prominent in Easthorpe life at that time.

Fouchers farmhouse itself fell to being no more than a cottage, though above the status of Hazells or Hoggets. The Joslin family occupied it for some years, succeeded in about 1860 by George Theedham, bailiff, his wife and three children. Theedham was from Copford, and was a descendant of the family of that name who for two or three hundred years inhabited Thedams Farm, just opposite Shemmings, till its absorption into the Sturgeon estate in 1779.

Scotties

The site of the mainly seventeenth century farmhouse of Scotties is so remarkable that it must be almost unique. It stands at the junction of no fewer than five parishes, Easthorpe, Feering and Messing together with detached parts of Great Birch and

Ancient Farmsteads

Marks Tey. The parish boundary of Easthorpe passes right through the house. The terrier of 1637 describes the division as "the part of the house which is only right hand of the entry, which entry is in Easthorpe, with the side of the foreyard of the orchard". It goes on to say that some twelve acres of "land and meadow" is also in Easthorpe.

As mentioned in Chapter 1, the name of Scotties is tantalising in these circumstances. It seems to have been known variously as Scottards and Scotlives, but whether "scot" here refers to some peculiar freedom from mediaeval obligations and duties, perhaps related to its strange parochial situation, does not appear. More prosaically the name may be simply a derivation of Scott. A William Scott, son of John and Mary, was born in Easthorpe in 1623, and Nathaniel in 1625. After this no Scotts appear in the parish records though isolated earlier references do appear: a "father Scot" is recorded as being buried in 1582, and "mother Scott" the following year. Earlier still, a Walter Scottard is mentioned under Marks Tey in the Lay Subsidy of 1327.

Scotties

Other than these, no probable references to the history of Scotties earlier than 1623 are discoverable, but with two interesting and very early exceptions. One of these is the purchase in 1260 for 26 marks by Saker or Sayer de Fering, holding of John de Saundford and Mathilda his wife, of one messuage with 24 acres in Easthorpe. This is only a possible reference and would not be considered at all in relation to Scotties without the second. The later reference, in 1284, is to the purchase by the same Sayer (or his son) and Eustacia his wife, from Thomas son of Thomas de la Chambre, of one messuage and 70 acres in Easthorpe and Feering. As the probable owner of nearby Hazells is known at this date and Scotties is the only farmstead with land extending into Feering, this is a likely reference: indeed, Fouchers seems to be the only other possibility. If this second reference is to Scotties, then the messuage in the first reference may have adjoined it, though the possibilities as to what holding it may have been become speculative. Sayer's son, Hugh, is mentioned in the Lay Subsidy of 1327.

The first indisputable reference to Scotties occurs in 1623, at which time it was being farmed with nearby Hazells. At that date Scotties was just one of a number of small farmsteads in the vicinity, and there is no particular reason why it should have survived when others have not. One such holding, for example, was known as Rawlins; this lay just outside the parish boundary in Feering, and was held by the Westons of Prested Hall, but was farmed with Scotties apparently from 1621 until

Ancient Farmsteads

partly leased away again at the end of the eighteenth century. Rawlins itself was "Rawlins and Salmons els Viners and Widows lands", which speaks of yet older and smaller holdings. Salmons appears to have been separate from Rawlins at one time, and to have been farmed by a family of the same name: the "Widow Salmon" who died in 1591 is the last known. Even as late as 1668 its separate identity was remembered, John Clarke holding Salmons while James Clarke held Scotties. Before 1700, however, as elsewhere in the parish, all this fragmentation had ceased.

The owners during the seventeenth century were the Clarkes, whose main residence was Fouchers (Easthorpe Green), and they have already been mentioned in connection with its history. Here it may be observed that they do not come out well from the records. They seem to have been at the centre of many disputes, although the rights and wrongs are no longer clear. The very first reference to a Clarke is a highway prosecution in 1611, when William Clarke "of Feering, having within the parish of Easthorpe a plowland", had not found on any of the "6 days appointed in June a wayne or draft" or an able person. This, of course, related to that troublesome hundred yards of the A12. By 1616 William Clarke is of Easthorpe, but offended against a statute by cutting down oaks "meet to be barked" and a Great Braxted carpenter, John Claydon, (the Clarkes were originally from that parish) took 21s from him in some sort of composition of the offence. This is an unusual prosecution at the date and it sounds as though Clarke had for some reason aroused particular local antagonism.

The occupiers of the farm in these years were the family of March or Marshe, every bit as turbulent as their landlords. Thomas March, after many offences over some thirty years, mostly resulting in injunctions to keep the peace, was at length committed to the house of correction in 1623. The immediate cause was that as "a haunter of taverns" he "failed to provide for his wife and family". Richard March, the next occupier, had given way to another William by the time William Clarke died in 1651. He was succeeded by the more peaceable and distinctly puritan family of Tibbald, Tibball or Theobald.

Several Tibbald wills survive. One of these, of Richard Tibbald in 1625, apparently long pre-dating their occupation of Scotties, leaves an annuity of 26s 8d, "a posted bedstead and the bed which he doth lie on", to Rachel his wife, provided that she makes no trouble about the division of his property. Rachel, dying as late as 1658 leaves a coat to the widow Emorie, presumably of Well Cottage, and various small items elsewhere. Thomas Tibball, in 1693, seems by comparison to have been quite well-to-do. His will was witnessed by his "good friend" Thomas Green, lord of the manor, and by Mary and Anne Green. He left his daughter Elizabeth "£100, one bedstead, one bolster, two pillows, two pillowbeers, a table, a cupboard, a rug, which are in the parlour chamber, and my best sheets...". To John Tibball, however, 30/- a quarter to be paid in the porch of the parish church, but — revealingly — not to his assigns; yet "if he marry then £100 at the discretion of Thomas Green"!

Meanwhile the Clarkes, back at their Great Braxted base, were not doing well. Scotties suffered a series of mortgages around 1700, eventually cleared in 1706 through the sale of other land. In effect James Clarke, aged about 30 at the time, sold Hazells to clear Scotties. In 1721, however, Scotties was sold to Sir William Luckyn of Messing, who in this way brought Scotties and Hazells back into a single ownership. Even so, Scotties, as one of the furthest flung pieces of the estate, was quickly split off

50

Ancient Farmsteads

again through a series of marriage settlements. It is soon found with Sarah Hucks, daughter of Joseph Hucks, who married the Rev. Anthony Cope in 1753 and who after his death became Mrs. Sarah Jackson when she married the Bishop of Kildare. She did not die until 1805, at which time Scotties was inherited by George Wegg, of the well-known Colchester family. His father, Samuel Wegg, of Lincolns Inn, is mentioned as the owner in 1806, but it was eventually sold to the Earl of Verulam in 1822, so going back to the head of the Luckyns of Messing. The Luckyns had changed their name to Grimston, and the third Viscount Grimston was created Earl of Verulam in 1790.

In 1720 the last John Tibball died, and from this date the farm was occupied by the widespread Eley family, originally from Feering and by this time based at Prested Hall in the south of that parish. During their time Scotties generally went with Hazells. William Eley farmed it (see Canfields) and Thomas Eley, who appears in the records as a determined and successful man, farmed it after William's death in 1798 and possibly earlier. Some part of the land he seems to have bought but other parts he rented. In 1835, during the agricultural difficulties of the time, it is described as having "a brewhouse, barn and a small old barn, and the land is foul". The Rounds considered purchasing it but decided not to make an offer. Thomas Eley, it appears, was having trouble with his rent in respect of some land owned by the Weggs; Lord Verulam continued to own the rest. Fifty years later this was still the case, but the owners today are uniformly the Sherwoods.

The last Eleys in the parish lived at Scotties. William Eley died in 1877, but his children continued to farm it; the last of them died in 1891. Most of the Eley tombs which stand together at the north east corner of Easthorpe churchyard are of Eleys from Scotties. The only remembrance of them today is that Scotties is recalled to have been known as Toops, or Tups, apparently the nickname of one of the last of the male Eleys, either William or his son John.

Hoggets

Hoggets is a house of mainly seventeenth century construction but raised and altered in the eighteenth century; a barn of similar date stands against it. Its siting is interesting. It stands at what seems to be a curious angle to the lane and very close to it, but this lane has changed its course and the house is in fact looking across what was once Porters Green.

Porters is one of a series of greens connected by the lane, a way of at least mediaeval origin. As mentioned in Chapter 1, it runs through Copford Green, Mulberry Green (anciently Crouches Land), Dawsons Green, Porters Green, Sandfordhall Green, Hardys Green. Most of these names date only from the eighteenth century and are traceable to local farmers, but there is no discoverable connection between the Porter family (of Messing and for a century of Badcocks) and the green that bears their name. It is possible that the allusion is a much earlier one; for example, a William Porter is mentioned at Marks Tey in 1327. The track beside Hoggets which led from the green passes against a long strip of land once described as waste and shown on old maps as woodland. Only one portion of this now remains, just before it is crossed by another track which starts at Dawsons Green and was once a throughway to Layer Marney.

It is interesting that Porters Green should directly adjoin one of the detached portions of the parish. This portion, in Hoggets' case, is about five acres in size,

Ancient Farmsteads

consisting of the house and garden and also a field, now absorbed into a larger one by the recent destruction of its ancient boundaries, into which the rear doors of the barn once opened. These five acres bore the name of Easthorpe Croft.

Prior to about 1640 Easthorpe Croft was owned by John Goodwin, and the earlier parts of the present house may possibly date from his time. This John Goodwin was the last of a family of some antiquity in Easthorpe. A John Goodwin senior was buying and selling land as early as 1417, and had several holdings in 1422, Hoggets apparently amongst them. There are several later references. A John Goodwin appears in the Lay Subsidy of 1524, for example, and was perhaps the John Goodwin who witnessed the will of John Vesye in the same year. At the same date John Goodwin senior witnessed the will of John Ardleigh of Flispes. The Goodwins may have inhabited Hoggets, but may equally have inhabited Penrils (see No Name), or indeed they may not have been resident in either: the family was widespread. For example, probate was granted for the will of a John Goodwin of Stanway in 1588.

Hoggets

In 1622 the last "John Goodwin the elder" of Easthorpe died, and on the death of his son, the last John Goodwin of all, the property passed to George Reade, a substantial farmer and landowner from Layer. He died in 1658 and his son, who inherited, in 1683. From him it passed to a nephew, but he sold it in 1687 to a man named Griffith, who almost immediately sold it again to John Chandler.

During the time of the first George Reade Easthorpe Croft was held by Thomas Reade, presumably a relation: this was so as early as 1636. His tenancy must have been short, however, because for most of this century the tenants were the Woodwards. Robert Woodward paid a twopenny rent in respect of "an encroachment", which is likely to have been the ploughing up of Porters Green itself, by William Woodward at

Ancient Farmsteads

about the time of the Civil War. The Woodward family can be traced as tenants for at least sixty years, and as Woodwards in the parish can, similarly to the Goodwins, be traced as far back as the Lay Subsidy of 1524 it is possible that their connection with Easthorpe Croft is equally long. They even achieved some success, as a Thomas Woodward of Easthorpe was admitted as a burgess of Colchester in 1549. The later Woodwards appear rarely in the records and the last mentions of them are in the registers, where Robert Woodward is stated to have married Mary Dell in 1667, and Thomas Woodward of Woodstock, Oxfordshire, to have been buried in 1668; a Robert Woodward and a John Woodward had houses in Birch at or immediately after this time. William Woodward, last Woodward occupier of Hoggets, is stated in 1671 to have died since the previous session of the manor court in 1663, but the very last Easthorpe record is that of Rebecca Woodward "of this parish" who married a Jacob Godfrey in 1671.

The land known as Hoggets was at this period quite separate from Easthorpe Croft, being a strip of twenty acres in front of the house along the eastern side of the lane to Sandfordhall Green. The earliest certain reference shows that it was owned by Mark Mott, the wealthy rector of Rayne, father of a later active Essex puritan of the same name. At the rector's death in 1630 he willed the land of Hoggets, together with the adjoining Whitehouse Farm, to his three daughters. The name at the time was Holdgates, but although a family called Holdgate existed in the district and even had land in Birch parish, no direct connection is traceable; they may possibly have been the owners previous to Mott. Mott's own connection with the parish, remote from his own and even more remote from his residence at Hadham, Hertfordshire, must have related to his friendship with John Clarke of Copford Hall, who was made overseer of his will. This will is to be found in the Greater London Record Office by virtue of its being proved in the Consistory Court of the Bishop of London. His bequests of a "silver toasting iron" and suchlike exotica together with various editions of the bible are of unusual interest.

Some time before 1663 Hoggets came into the possession of John Dawes, who had succeeded John Ludgate as sequestrating minister of Great Birch in 1653. He was ejected in 1660 and it is not known where he went; other than his continued ownership of Hoggets nothing seems to be traceable of him. His land was certainly tenanted in 1663, but the name of the tenant is only half-written in the manorial records. It is possibly intended for John Arger, a well-known puritan clergyman who after his ejection from Braintree retired to Copford until his death in 1679 (he was licensed there in 1672). John Dawes was still the owner as late as 1685, but shortly after this the land passed to the owner of Easthorpe Croft, that is to John Chandler, who by 1687 was certainly the owner of both. The farm thus became of viable size and was thenceforth known as Hoggets.

John Chandler appears to have been also of a puritan persuasion. By trade he was a wheelwright, though it is not clear whether his yard was in the village, where one certainly existed a hundred years later, or near Heckfordbridge, where a large wheelwright's shop existed for several centuries, or even in Birch. He owned a few small pieces of land elsewhere, but it is doubtful whether he personally farmed even Hoggets itself, though he certainly lived at the house. It is known that in 1689 the land was being farmed by William Thedam, whose farm stood next to Shemmings pond and whose land therefore adjoined that of Hoggets.

Ancient Farmsteads

John Chandler's personal life must have been a sad one. His first appearance in the records is in 1671, at which time he was presumably already living in the house at Easthorpe Croft. In this year his wife Margaret and a child of the same name were buried in Easthorpe churchyard. He quickly remarried a certain Martha Bonnet, who was not local, and successive children were born to them: John, 1674, then three Marthas in 1678, 1682 and 1685, but all died in early infancy. Hoggets never had a well, and perhaps was not a healthy house.

John Chandler himself died in 1707 and left an interesting will. Martha was still alive, and he desired to be buried near his dead children in Easthorpe churchyard. Most of his relatives were at Ridgewell or Halstead, where he actually owned a windmill. His property was to be split up amongst many relations, and his "tenement with yard and courtyard now in the occupation of myself and the trustees of the poor of Birch Magna", was to be sold. It is possible that Martha may have continued to live at Hoggets, as she was described as "of this parish" when buried at Easthorpe in 1713.

Who owned Hoggets during the next few years is mysterious. The Manor Court did not know in 1711 or even as late as 1727. Soon after this, however, it was in the possession of John Eley, and the various changes to the structure of the house may have been undertaken by him. The Eleys were a Feering family but during the eighteenth century spread across Easthorpe very rapidly. The John Eley who owned Hoggets was almost certainly the John Eley who owned Prested Hall and who had prospered so greatly as to have some pretensions to being a gentleman. This John Eley married as his second wife a Mary Barnard in 1759. He was her third husband, her first being a Thomas Green, possibly a distant relative of the last resident Easthorpe lord of the manor. When John Eley died in 1765 his elder son, another John, inherited his lands, but younger brother William received only £10. This William may have been the William Eley mentioned in the history of Canfields.

During the time of the elder John Eley Hoggets was tenanted by Thomas Garrard who had entered upon the tenancy before 1751. He and his wife Martha had three children, but the eldest died, and when Thomas himself died in 1769 his wife seems to have given up the tenancy. John Eley thereupon soon afterwards made over the farm to William Eley; this William was probably his younger brother, but the name William was so popular in the Eley family that it is impossible to be certain. The farm was certainly owner-occupied thereafter, and John Eley himself died in 1776.

Two William Eleys are distinguished in the records as "William Eley of Easthorpe" and "William Eley of Birch". The William Eley of Hoggets was the latter, because most of his land was in that parish. Disappointingly little of him is known, considering that he farmed it until 1809, but his wife Mary was probably a Turnage, a family farming and owning some fields near Canfields. When William sold Hoggets, or at about that time, it appears that he became owner of Canfields; his son John, 1782-1855, certainly owned it at the time the Tithe Map was drawn up. At the same time his second son Isaac 1791-1870, was farming it. Daniel, the third son, 1797-1869, lived obscurely in Birch William's tomb may be seen in the churchyard (he died in 1825 at the age of 79), as may those of his three sons.

Hoggets cannot have been a prosperous holding, being under thirty acres, and when it passed to George Eley, presumably a relation of William, he put it up for auction only two years later. The notice in the Essex Herald of 26th July, 1811, says

Ancient Farmsteads

that it is to be sold by auction by Matthews and Son, on Thursday, 1st August, at the Chapel Inn, Coggeshall, at 5 o'clock of the afternoon in one lot. It consisted of "all that comfortable dwelling house, substantial barn, stable, cowhouse, cartlodge, and other outbuildings, with the yards, gardens and appurtenances, and twenty six acres of sound, good and productive arable land, all freehold, lying very compact, and in the occupation of Mr. George Eley the proprietor, who will show the premises on application to him upon the same".

The purchaser was William Hutley, of a Bradwell family. The Hutleys were blacksmiths in Feering, Birch, Rivenhall and elsewhere, and William Hutley seems to have followed the same trade himself while buying various pieces of land over the years. In 1817 he purchased Little Badcocks, which he leased out, and it is most unlikely that he ever lived at Hoggets. Indeed, it is probable that it was as early as this that the house was partitioned off into the three cottages or "lets" which it certainly soon afterwards became. The land itself was farmed by William Wade, who eventually leased Great Badcocks, and he may have lived at Hoggets for a time. Although William Hutley did not die till 1855, he sold the house and land to Robert Levett of Beckingham Hall in 1826, Hutley continuing to be recorded as occupier till his death. The Levetts were originally a Coggeshall family and Robert Levett was at this time building up a considerable estate.

After Hutley's death Levett seems to have farmed Hoggets directly from Beckingham Hall, and shortly before his own death it was farmed still as part of Beckingham Hall by Joseph Powell. Hoggets must have been a somewhat inconvenient piece of land at this period, as the erstwhile Sturgeon estates, which included the old Thedams Farm, were still in the hands of the descendants of one of his daughters, and formed a block which separated Hoggets from Beckingham Hall.

The trustees of Robert Levett's estate eventually sold out in 1881 to the Impey estate, from which it was several miles separated, and it was not till 1903 that Hoggets at last became part of the great Round estate of which it had long logically been part. It lay then and still lies just within its western border. The estate at length converted the cottages back into a single dwelling, and they were sold off as a single residence in 1964.

Canfields

The earliest parts of the house of Canfields are seventeenth century, but it was substantially altered and renovated in both the eighteenth and the nineteenth centuries. It stands in one of the three southern detached areas of the parish, about six acres in extent. Its earliest known name is Cawens, by which it was called when John Wright leased it in 1544, but late in the same century references occur to Carbins Lane. The house was still referred to as Cawens in as late as 1637, but in 1642 a field adjacent to it was known as Canfield, presumably a contraction of Cawenfield, and this name was transferred to the house.

Adjacent to Canfields but apparently held or owned separately — or at least not known as Cawens — was land called variously Turners or Beards or Bards, lying in Easthorpe, Messing and the two Birches. John Daniel of Messing, referred to under Hazells, Badcocks and Scotties, leased Turners to Anthony Stonard or Stonnard in 1568. From Daniel the ownership passed in 1582, perhaps after a brief ownership by a

55

Ancient Farmsteads

Thomas Biggs of London, to Peter Thompson of London, woodmonger, but in 1589 it was sold again to Philip Blosse, who had been the occupier since Stonard's death. The

Canfields

Blosse family built up their holding in the area through a series of minor purchases, but may have been adversely affected by the Civil War; at all events, their property was split up again by John Blosse in the early 1640's, Canfields itself going to William Durrant of St. Peters, Colchester.

It is not certain who occupied Canfields at this period, though the Stonards are the most likely family as they continue to appear in the parish records throughout. If so they probably owned Cawens (the house) and tenanted Canfields (the farm), as these holdings are not subsequently found separated. The death of John Stonard senior occurred in 1597, the marriage of two other Johns occurring one in that year and one the year before. Children appear thereafter with frequency. One of the two John Stonards is likely to have farmed Winnings (see Chapter 7), and he is probably the "old Stonard" who died in 1639. The other John Stonard certainly died in 1632, and in 163 the occupier of Canfields was a William Levett.

The history of Canfields is then in complete obscurity until it is found in the possession of John Stilliman at his death in 1699. He is also referred to as the owner of Crossfield, a field adjacent to Poynants, the house which stood at the end of the track opposite Hellens Farm until its demolition in 1956 or thereabouts. For the next half century, until Charles Gray became the owner in 1746, the history of the ownership of Canfields is a series of careful protections under successive marriage settlements as it descended in the female line. One of the husbands from whom it was thus protected had been for a time a part owner: this was William Potter, whose family soon

Ancient Farmsteads

afterwards began their long connection with nearby Winterfloods. By the time Charles Gray purchased it, the owners were a certain William Hill and Elizabeth his wife. Charles Gray, whose name appears in several Easthorpe house histories, was busy building up what was to become the Round estate, but towards the end of the century the further flung properties were disposed of again in favour of consolidating the estate by purchases nearer home. Canfields was one of these remoter properties, but for some reason the Rounds held on to one part of their holding.

The next owner represented another expanding estate, being John Eley of Prested Hall; he already owned Hoggets. Whether this was John Eley the father or John Eley the son, however, is uncertain; it can be said only that by 1780 it was in the hands of the Eleys. The occupier in the early years of Charles Gray appears to have been John May, and if so this will have been before his tenancy of Fouchers in 1756. Thereafter the name of Thomas Turnage appears in connection with the property, but it may be that he farmed only certain fields. The tenant for all the latter part of the century was Daniel Gilder senior, who farmed there at least forty years and possibly much longer. His death did not occur till 1809, when he was 85 and living with his elder son at Birch. Although Gilder's age may not seem remarkable, it is almost unparallelled in Easthorpe, where longevity does not seem to have been common. His will survives, and his tomb is still visible in the parish churchyard, though today it lies flat and is quickly deteriorating.

After the lease of Canfields house ran out the Eleys farmed it themselves; this seems to have been some time during the 1780's. That part of the property still owned by the Rounds, however, remained with them. Daniel Gilder farmed it, then Thomas Gilder, and then briefly (from 1804) Thomas and John Turnage, but soon afterwards all was absorbed into the Eley ownership. Old Daniel continued to regard Easthorpe as his parish, and was buried there though "of Birch". What is more, Daniel and Elizabeth Gilder, his grandchildren, described as "twin infants from Birch", were buried in Easthorpe two years before him, no doubt for the same reason.

The most interesting story of Canfields is that of William Eley, the younger brother of John, who died in 1798. He was 60 at the time and churchwarden. He farmed Scotties and Hazells (after 1779) as well as Canfields, and was left only £10 in his father's will, perhaps because he was considered sufficiently prosperous. He had married his wife, Susannah May from Badcocks, when he was only 18 and she was 21. Their first child, William, died in infancy in 1759 and a second son John died in 1766, but their daughter Susannah survived, and so did a second son William. Susannah the younger married William Moore of Pebmarsh in 1783 and her signature can be seen in the parish register: they had one son, William. The William who was this Susannah's brother was also married, to Elizabeth Turrell, and they had a daughter, another Elizabeth. This must have seemed very satisfactory to William Eley senior, but in the two years before 1798 all but Elizabeth and the two grandchildren died. William's consequent anxiety comes out clearly in his will as he also lay dying, in 1798. The farm was left to Elizabeth, his daughter-in-law. She was "to carry on the business of the farm" and bring up the children, but realising how difficult this would be for her he exhorted his nephew, Thomas Eley of Feering, to assist. William Eley of nearby Hoggets may have helped; he did at least take some interest as he owned the farm a few years later.

Elizabeth did in fact accomplish her task successfully, and yet more Eleys survived

Ancient Farmsteads

to farm in the area after her time. In 1840 John Eley, William's son, owned part of Canfields and Isaac Eley farmed it. Thomas Eley owned the other part, and farmed himself together with Hazells and part of Scotties. Another Thomas Eley lived at Hunts, now the 'No Name', and kept the shop. Several other Eleys farmed smaller pieces of land in the neighbourhood. Young William Moore, one of the grandchildren of William Eley, appears to have taken the name William Eley and then to have left the district, but there are so many William Eleys that it is difficult to be sure. Your Elizabeth Eley, the other grandchild, is the Elizabeth who died in 1833 and whose tomb can still be seen in the churchyard.

The Eleys have far more tombstones in the parish churchyard than any other Easthorpe family, though many of them were born outside the parish boundary. They seem to have delighted in the confusion caused by their frequent use of the same christian names — notably John, Elizabeth and William. Two tombstones stand next to each other commemorating Williams, and even though their deaths were fifty years apart they bear the same text. Several of the stones have connections with Canfields and they include those of the last Eley inhabitants. Isaac died in 1870, his wife Rhoda in 1874 at the age of 89, and their son Thomas predeceased them in 1861.

Winterfloods, as it was

Winterfloods

Winterfloods is a late sixteenth century house rather drastically modified and rebuilt recent years. An adjacent and attractive contemporary barn has also been demolished. The deplorable 'restoration' of Well Cottage (which saddens the present owners), the dereliction of Flispes, and the spoliation of Winterfloods are the three most damaging architectural events in the parish within the last half century: all could have been avoided.

The history of Winterfloods is disappointingly obscure, although a Ralph Winterflod appears in the Assize Rolls as early as 1280; thereafter there seems to only one indubitable reference (in 1430) till the terrier of 1637 already mentioned in connection with other houses. Winterfloods lies right on the edge of yet another of the detached portions of the parish, and the terrier well describes the peculiarity of the site: "Item, the house called Winterfloods, half the house southward with half the yard, half the orchard with two or three acres of land in Easthorpe". The name itself is descriptive of the once waterlogged condition of land in the area during the winter. Well Lane, a little nearer the village, is even today flooded across for many days at a time, and Winterfloods farmhouse stands barely above the saturation mark.

Little can be said with certainty of Winterfloods till as late as 1665, when it was owned by Hezekiah Dowsett of Messing. Before this it is possible to deduce probabilities by elimination of householders known to have lived elsewhere, but no more. It is possible, even probable, for example, that John Shelton was of Winterfloods at the time of the Lay Subsidy of 1524, but it cannot be proved. Winterfloods is likely to have passed through many hands, for it is conspicuous that where a 'most probable' occupier of Winterfloods can be surmised it is almost always one of the more fleeting names of the village. Even as late as the seventeenth century confidence can be little greater: the Norris family certainly occupied either Winterfloods or Well Cottage during the Commonwealth period but, unfortunately for the history of Winterfloods, Well Cottage is much the more likely of the two.

The most probable occupiers during the middle years of the seventeenth century are the Theobald or Tibbald family, referred to under Scotties, Hazells and Flispes, succeeded thereafter by one or other of the Deamons or Damyons (see Spicers). By 1698, and probably even by 1682 from analogies with other property, Winterfloods had passed into the hands of Obadiah Paul, Easthorpe's land-dealing rector. In 1708 it was owned by John Rawlins, but as so often when land was owned by Paul it is uncertain how and where the transfer of ownership took place. By his will of that year Winterfloods was left to his wife, Catherine, then after her death to his daughters Catherine and Elizabeth, or in the event of their death to his two sons. Widow Catherine did not die till 1725, by which time both her sons and her daughter Catherine were already dead. Winterfloods therefore passed to Elizabeth and her husband Andrew Harrington. From them it quickly passed to Thomas Holgrave, but in 1733 was sold by him to William Miles of Messing, butcher, the same man mentioned in the history of Great Guildhouse.

Certainly in 1707, and no doubt from some time earlier, Winterfloods was occupied by John Blowers, who died in 1737, and he was succeeded by Thomas Blowers who died in 1776. Because the records of Tibbald and Damyon occupiers are so doubtful it is tempting to speculate that the "mansion house" (a term normally used of a yeoman-style farmhouse) of an earlier John Blowers of Easthorpe, forcibly entered in 1586 and not otherwise identifiable, was in fact Winterfloods, and that the occupiers had throughout continued in the line of Blower. Unfortunately there is no proof of this at all, and even after the Damyons the family of Potter are more likely Restoration occupiers than the Blowers. Indeed, in the sixteenth century the occupiers may equally well have been the Currye family, who make frequent appearances in the records — a Richard Currye was "beaten" at the self-same 1586 breaking and entering. This could be explained by supposing that the Curryes were undertenants of the Blowers, but that again is mere speculation.

Ancient Farmsteads

From the son of William Miles Winterfloods passed to Abraham de Horne, given as owner in 1765, and then successively through Thomas and George de Horne to John described in 1800 as a cheesemonger of Stepney. The de Hornes were actually a good deal wealthier than that implies, and they held Winterfloods together with other property in the neighbourhood for over a century. For example, George de Horne was tenant of Stanway Hall at his death in 1771. They also appear to have had some earlier connection in the district, though the nature of this is obscure. The Colchester Oath Book refers to a deed of 1621 involving a childless Abraham de Horne of London cheesemaker, son of George de Horne, late of London, tailor.

Throughout the ownership of the de Hornes, after the death of Thomas Blowers in 1776, the tenants were the Potter family, mostly Williams and Daniels. A Daniel was farming it at the time of the tithe redemption map of 1840. The Potters were widely spread in the area, and William was the preferred family name. In 1840 an entirely different William Potter farmed Hall Farm, but his relationship if any to the William Potter of Winterfloods is not clear. Subsequently Winterfloods was farmed by the Powells. John Powell, probably the grandson of Henry Powell of Fouchers (Easthorpe Green) was under notice to quit in 1878.

Chapter Six
THREE VILLAGE HOUSES, PAST AND PRESENT

No Name Public House
The fabric of the No Name is predominantly seventeenth century, but as with so many public houses the ground floor architecture is now either falsified or incomprehensible. The licence dates only from very recent years, the village having no public house from the time of the delicensing of the Bell until after the Second World War. The No Name operated as a private club until granted a full licence. Before being called the No Name it was Yew Tree Cottage; the stump of that yew tree, cut down well within living memory, can still be seen. As Yew Tree Cottage it had a small barn or shed at the corner opposite Well Cottage: the entrance to Well Lane was once much narrower than presently appears.

The No Name

Yew Tree Cottage was of course not the original name: for two or three hundred years its name was Hunts, before that Penrils or Goodwins, and its site makes a very early origin seem probable. Rather surprisingly, there seems to be no record of who 'Hunt' was. It can only be supposed that someone of that name briefly occupied the house during the poorly recorded period of the Civil War, for the name Hunts was certainly in use at the end of the century. The only recorded instance of the name Hunt in the parish occurs in connection with St. Johns Garden (see Chapter 7), which was "unjustly seized" by a certain Hugh Hunt in about 1700.

Penrils, the earlier name, is similarly of uncertain origin. It may be an error for the more likely sounding name of Pevrils or Peverills, and since Peverills do indeed occur in the parish registers before 1600 they must be regarded as likely occupants: the last

Three Village houses, past and present

such reference is to a Thomas Peverill who made his mark as churchwarden in 1598, but various of his children are recorded in earlier years. The Goodwins were thus perhaps the family before the Peverills: they were known in the parish for at least two hundred years, and various references to them have been noted under Hoggets. The Goodwins were in fact just as common in Birch, where they had a particular connection with a farm known as Goodwins or Kings near Beckingham Hall. Although the nature of the link between the Goodwins and the No Name cannot be determined exactly, it is not unreasonable to suppose that one or other of the two Goodwins referred to in the Lay Subsidy of 1524 was resident at that time.

The first detailed reference to the property occurs in the will of Robert Ham, who died in 1604. He resided at the No Name — or Penrils or Goodwins as it was then known — and the various scattered fields he farmed from it are noted. They lay in the east of the parish and stretched as far as Crowches Land (Mulberry Green). How long he had been there, or from whom he had purchased it, is not known. He may perhaps not have been there long, as Hams do not make earlier appearances in the records and his brother was from Chappel; this would of course fit the supposed Peverill connection.

Robert Ham left Goodwins to his wife Margaret, but it was leased from her by Thomas Ham, most probably the same Thomas who was Robert's brother from Chappel. After his death and that of Margaret it passed to Thomas's son, another Thomas, who was still residing and farming in 1637. When it left his possession is not known, but it may be at this period that the mysterious Hunt was in residence. Even so references to "land farmed now or lately by Thomas Ham" occur as late as 1660.

After the Restoration the names of owners and occupiers remain uncertain, though they can be narrowed down to a very few possibilities. The most likely connection by far is with Richard Parker, whose history is recorded under Great Guildhouse. Richard certainly paid the quit rent for Hunts in 1698, and it is a reasonable presumption that he was the same Richard Parker shown in all the earlier hearth taxes against a property which, by assigning all the other entries against likely residents, can again be shown to be most probably Hunts. In this case he may have succeeded Hunt.

Early in the eighteenth century, and certainly soon after 1710, Hunts was occupied by the family of Chinnery, but they did not own it. Of the ownership it can only be said that at the time the Chinnerys first appear in the records the ownership was with William Miles of Messing (see Great Guildhouse) and that on his death in 1737 he left to James Miles, his son. From James it passed to his brother Edward, who held it until his own death in 1763. His niece Mary, who inherited, had first married a certain John Garmond, and had in fact received Flanders and Georges Croft from William Miles in her own right. By the time of her uncle's death, however, John Garmond was dead and she was already remarried to Matthew Edwards. From him it seems quickly to have passed to James Edwards of Birch, possibly Matthew's brother, but in 1768 William Chinnery, the occupier, became owner in his own right.

Chinnery was in that year described as resident in Easthorpe but having freehold land elsewhere. His personal connection with Hunts dates to at least as early as 1756. Hunts in Chinnery's time was the village shop, so presumably the farm had in common with so many others been deemed unviable by about 1700. Chinnery never owned the land and is not known to have farmed it. His own title was "chandler", and he was

62

Three Village houses, past and present

visited by the weights and measures inspectors in 1777. A couple of attempts to set up a rival chandlery in the village were made during the same century but soon failed. William Chinnery is the subject of a curious entry in the accounts of the churchwardens of Great Birch who incurred expenses "to going after William Chinnery three days with a horse". Sadly, we do not know why.

William Chinnery died in 1783, and his now nearly illegible tombstone can still be seen in the churchyard near the porch, next to the tombs of the John Osbornes of Hall Farm. Its positioning is presumably the result of the marriage of his widow, Catherine, to the second John Osborne in the following year. John Osborne made his will on 17th January, 1784, just before his marriage, and died late in 1785. By its terms Catherine received nothing, his lands at Wormingford and indeed everything else going to his son, another John, who farmed at Wigborough. The register states that Catherine was living at Rettendon till the time of her own burial at Easthorpe at the age of 85 in 1808, a year after the burial in the same churchyard of the last John Osborne.

John Osborne would have been well aware when he married Catherine that she had sufficient property of her own, and this is probably why he omitted to provide for her. She continued to own Hunts and the shop for some years after John Osborne's death; it appears that during this entire period the occupier was Daniel Rayment, who held it until he died in 1794. At about this time Catherine sold the property to William Osborne, presumably a relation of her second husband: he, with his wife Margaret, had had two sons named William, each of whom died within a few days of birth in 1758 and 1759 respectively. After Daniel Rayment the occupier, and no doubt the shopkeeper, was James Edwards — perhaps the same as the earlier James, or his son.

About the year 1805 Hunts was bought by Thomas Oddy, blacksmith, owner of Well Cottage, and the ownership long continued in that family. In 1827 Thomas Eley became shopkeeper and was found there as "grocer" for many years; he continued to keep it into his eighties, assisted by a wife even older than himself. The shop property appears to have been split into two lets, however, as the village shoemaker, James Everett, resided there with them for at least thirty years.

The shop continued after the Eley's time and is remembered in more recent years for a series of colourful owners. When the property became the No Name public house the shop declined to an off-licence and subsequently was completely absorbed into the bar-room.

Well Cottage

Well Cottage stands conspicuously in the centre of the village, and its fabric is in origin a fifteenth century hall house. A dragon beam suggests a jetty at both front and side, but the house was so drastically reconstructed a few years ago that all other internal evidence must be treated with caution. Before this reconstruction its exterior timbers were plastered, and old photographs show it to have had a picturesque appearance. During repairs, when the plaster was removed, a sixteenth century shop front was revealed on the end facing the church (windowless in the illustration).

The well from which the house takes its present name still exists, its waters coming from one of several springs. Within living recollection the well stood open to the lane so that all villagers could use it, and when it was enclosed the gate in the fence was put there so that access could continue. Almost opposite the well a pair of small labourers'

Three Village houses, past and present

Well Cottage, as it was

cottages stood until 1922, but these do not seem to have been of ancient construction or origin.

Well Cottage was not the first name of the house. In the seventeenth century, and presumably earlier, it was known as Crosse House; the present garden was Well Close. Although this may just possibly denote an ecclesiastical origin, for the house is opposite the church and its land was glebe, such a name in Essex usually refers to a crossroads. The modern lane to the north, leading to Little Birch Holt, leaves the Roman Road some seventy yards away, but it is quite possible that at one time its beginning was opposite to Well Lane, following the edge of the churchyard. Indeed, a footpath is remembered to have followed just this route. Unfortunately no old map of the village centre exists so the point cannot be settled; no map was made because the field edge such a path would have followed was not estate land but glebe. To one side of the same small field, against the road, stood a cottage used for many years as the village school, which closed in 1898. If a section of lane did exist opposite Well Lane it may well be that known around 1600 as Bredlesse Street.

Well Cottage is strongly associated with the family of Emorie or Amorie; they owned it for two centuries and occupied it too for most of that time. Right from the beginning of the parish register the Emories figure prominently — indeed the very first reference in it is to the baptism of John Emorie son of John Emorie and Alice his wife — but there is no mention of the name in the Lay Subsidy of 1524 even though the house certainly existed at that date. The Emories were therefore probably not its builders. Disappointingly few Amorie wills exist, although that of John Amorie in 1595 describes him merely as a "labourer", which was probably accurate enough: at no time is there any evidence of prosperity. This same John Amorie, the first of whom we have certain knowledge, died in 1596, and his son Richard inherited. In 1620 William Amorie, latest of a long series of sons of Richard, was born. In 1621 Richard's mother "Widow Amorie", died, and Richard himself later the same year. In 1622 Lawrence Amorie, son of the new "Widow Amorie", was born.

Three Village houses, past and present

In 1646 a John Amorie confirmed that William Porter had not repaired the churchyard fence, but all other references concerning this John Amorie refer to him as being of Copford, and no Amorie appears in the Hearth Tax of 1662. The occupiers at this period must be sought elsewhere, and the most likely during the Commonwealth are the Norris family. When their residence began is not clear: "Old Norris" died and was buried in 1638 but does not appear to have been resident in Well Cottage in 1636. The date of its ending presents fewer problems: Arthur Norris does not appear again in Easthorpe after 1662 and Arthur Norris "of Colchester" was buried in Easthorpe churchyard in 1668. As the Easthorpe references to Amories appear again at the same time, it seems that after the Commonwealth, between 1662 and 1668, they returned to residence.

Richard Amorie's grandson John, the eldest son of the John mentioned in 1646, was married to a certain Grace just before 1660. The last John Amorie, who apparently never married, was born to them in that year. Grace died soon after the birth and John senior seems to have remarried, for a daughter Abigail was born to John and Alice in 1670. It may be that in later years the Amories went back to Copford once again, as Easthorpe records of them cease while Copford records continue. It is unlikely that the last John Amorie lived in Easthorpe at all, for the records are silent about him, and it is possible, though it cannot be proved, that from the 1670's onwards the family of Goodall resided. A number of children were born to them in the 1670's and '80's, but eventually moved away; John Goodall, "the church clerk and ancient inhabitant of the parish", died in 1713.

Well Cottage was never a large farm. In 1637 John Amorie of Copford had "the cottage with six acres"; it was therefore the typically sized small holding of the parish and compares in this respect with several other of the older holdings. Like them too, it seems to have lost its land at the end of the seventeenth century, perhaps when the Amories went back to Copford. John Amorie the last still held Well Cottage in 1698, but twenty years or so later, and certainly before his death in 1727, the owner was a certain Robert Moreton, freeholder in 1722 and still resident in 1734. Robert Moreton's wife Elizabeth died in 1738 and he married a widow, Sarah Rayner, the same year. From Moreton it passed in about 1740 to Solomon Oddy.

The Oddys were the Easthorpe blacksmiths until succeeded by the Hutleys in the nineteenth century. They themselves succeeded the Searles, resident in Easthorpe for many years; as the Searles are recorded as blacksmiths "of Little Birch" they no doubt kept the Bell Public House like the Oddys after them. An unusual prosecution occurred in 1662 when Thomas Oddy, blacksmith, was fined for working as a baker without having been apprenticed to it, but Easthorpe trade must always have been scanty and perhaps he thought it a pity to see the forge fire go to waste. He was certainly unfortunate, being the victim of an informer called Edward Farrell, who was rewarded for similar prosecutions of some thirty people in the area around this time. It was probably the same Thomas who paid Ship Money in 1636, shortly after coming to Easthorpe: he would at this time certainly have lived at the Bell close to the Smithy.

It is doubtful whether the Oddys ever resided at Well Cottage. It is far more probable that after purchasing it they promptly divided it into the two or even three lets which it certainly was from the mid eighteenth century till recent times. Their ownership was accordingly uneventful, the property descending in the family even after they had left the village. In 1833 James Oddy of Runwell mortgaged Well Cottage

65

Three Village houses, past and present

and the cottages opposite the well, though not the No Name, which he also owned. The mortgaged properties were stated to be in the occupation of Samuel Christmas, Jame Polley, James Fisher and William Moss. Well Cottage did not finally pass out of the hands of the Oddys till 1884, when it was sold by Solomon Oddy of Rettendon to Jame Edwards, then rector of Easthorpe. When he left the parish four years later he sold it to Walter Siggers, whereafter it passed through several ownerships. Amongst the tenant occupying the property occur such well-known village names as Brazier, Fletcher Seabrook, Polley and Lappage.

The only earlier tenants worthy of special note are the family of Christmas. The lived in the cottage for at least three generations (a Samuel Christmas dying there in 1781) and one of their number, though only a labourer, is commemorated by handsome tombstone which now lies sadly flattened and deteriorating in th churchyard. Its legend is worth reproducing in full: "Samuel Christmas, died 1844 aged 79. He was for upwards of forty years parish clerk, and for more than fifteen i the service of John Hallward, Rector of this Parish, by whom this stone is erected i testimony of respect and regard for an honest man and a sincere and humble Christiar He was one who feared God and regarded man. Reader, go and do thou likewise". Th rector who wrote this touching tribute left the parish the same year.

Great Guildhouse
The Great Guildhouse, which stood against the "No Name" where Onslow Cottage now stand, is one of the mysteries of Easthorpe. The puzzle is the origin of its name

There are several possibilities. One is that it is derived from the name Guilde borough. In the eighteenth century the quatrefoil window in the south wall of the nav of the church (set beneath a low arch itself of mysterious purpose) contained four coa of arms, one of which was that of the family of Guildesborough. That family originate at Wennington, near Rainham, but the only connection with the village or the lords the manor that can be traced is the doubtful coincidence that when in 1389 Sir Joh Guildesborough conveyed his manor of Wennington Hall to trustees, Clement Spic transferred all his rights in that manor likewise: the family of Spice or Spicer had i arms in the same quatrefoil.

A second possibility is that it had some relation to the Guild of St. Helen. This gui arose from the Crutched Friars, Colchester, which was first a convent, or a hospita next a free chapel, or hospital; and finally a church. Its function seems to have been charity for poor people. The Guild of St. Helen was founded in the chapel in 1409, a both chapel and hospital eventually came into the possession of the guardians of tl guild. There is a record of the Crutched Friars themselves being turned out of the house some time before 1490, but where they went does not appear. Morant h several yearly accounts of the revenues of this guild, and amongst them references "five acres of land in Copford" and "seven acres in Great Birch or Easthorpe". Some this land was at Mulberry Green, which until Thomas Mulberry arrived in 1709 w always known as Crouches Land. This, however, does not account for their land Easthorpe and a connection is possible.

The third possibility is the most intriguing and also the most likely; this is that the was a local and short-lived guild of St. Mary. There are so many records of sm religious guilds in Essex, though many of them identifiable only from a sing

Three Village houses, past and present

reference, that it seems that few villages eventually were without one. There was one dedicated to Corpus Christi at nearby Feering, for example, and another at Great Birch. The small size of the village would seem to have been no obstacle: for example, in 1522 at Great Henny Thomas Guyblon left his house called Fidlers to the Guild of St. John Baptist "to be a Guylde Hall for ever". At Birch the Lay Subsidy of 1524 mentions in a separate paragraph of the assessment "The stock of our lady guylde in the hands of John Bushe, warden". In the county generally, some of the guilds which certainly owned property can be identified by valuations at the Reformation, but not all, and there are many deeds of sale which seem to refer to guild property. Even so, records are so scarce that it can be shown that lack of reference to a valuation is no proof of non-existence.

There is in fact some circumstantial evidence that Easthorpe did have a late guild. The story of this evidence begins in 1524, the year of the Lay Subsidy return. In this year John and Nicholas Goodwin, one at least of them probably from Hunts (No Name), next door to the Guildhouse, are recorded for the parish. So too is a William Vesye at the same valuation as Goodwin (£6) and so is Widow Parker, rated at 40s goods, and Robert Parker — who at 20s earnings is the only resident of the parish rated on this less usual basis. Where the Parkers lived at this time is uncertain, but by elimination it can be shown that there is a reasonable possibility that the Vesyes lived at the Guildhouse or whatever it was then called. The later evidence bears out this assumption.

In that same year of 1524 William Vesye died. Amongst the witnesses to his short will is John Goodwin, and there is a reference to "Thomas Parker, my godson". Vesye died sufficiently old to refer to grandchildren, but his will deals almost solely with one subject: his son-in-law Robert Grey was to pay 6s 8d to Alice, William's wife, of the 18/-that was owed. If he did, he was to be forgiven the rest, but if not then it was to be recovered "by suite and press of law". As to his property, if Robert was "kind, diligent and loving" to Alice and did not run off with the furniture then he was to have everything after her death, but if not then Alice should dispose of all "for the health of our souls and for all christian souls".

We hear no more until the death of Alice in 1532, but from her short and pious will it appears that her relations with Robert Grey had not gone well. Alice calls in William Vesye, certainly not her natural son so probably her husband's son by a previous marriage, to act as executor. After the customary bequest to "Powles Church" (St. Paul's), and another for an obit, Alice says "the residue of all my goods movable and immovable I give and bequeathe to William Vesye aforesaid, he to dispose of them for the weale of my soule as shall beseem him best upon the day and year above specified" (i.e. the date of the will or her death). No more is heard of this William, but one of the most obvious ways of carrying out both this will and that of his father would have been to set up, or further endow, a village Lady Guild through gift of the dwelling-house or the rented revenues from it.

In a visitation report of 1543 occurs the only apparent direct reference to a guild in the village: "Robert Parker oweth 5 nobles to our lady guild". This must have been the widow's son of 1524, and from his earlier connections it seems quite possible that he was resident in the Guildhouse but had failed to pay the rent. At all events, records of the Parkers are frequent from this time.

In 1552, in the Colchester Oath Book, there are references connecting the Parkers

Three Village houses, past and present

with John Kingston, rector of Easthorpe. In that year there is an "obligation, with condition of Robert Parker of Easthorpe" to Kingston, and later a deed. In the same year there is a release of Thomas Parker, "son and heir of John Parker late of Feering son and heir of Alice wife of Michael Parker (and after his death wife of William Vesey) daughter of Richard Heering". From the damaged introduction to the inventory of the church goods in 1552 it can be inferred that Thomas Parker was churchwarden in that year. It appears that Thomas Parker was releasing himself from his responsibilities, but it is not entirely clear whether Kingston is arranging a sale or a lease with Robert Parker. Kingston himself did own Winnings at the time (see Chapter 7) and after his death left it as a charity. Concern from Kingston about the Guildhouse would be in character.

During the latter part of the sixteenth century there occur a few rather mysterious references to a messuage called Calveswick ad Guildhall. Morant refers to it erroneously, as "Colverwicke alias Guildhall". This messuage was owned by Robert Spring and after his death in 1570 by his widow Joan, then later again by her son and heir Thomas Perient, already referred to under the history of Easthorpe Hall. Calveswick is stated to be in Little Birch and partly in Great Birch and Copford; Birch Guildhall lay close to Great Birch Church, and in the absence of positive evidence it must be presumed to have no connection with the Easthorpe Great Guildhouse.

The first mention of "Great Guildhouse" under that name occurs in 1571 and is a surprising one as it occurs in the will of John Hewer. He was much the wealthiest man in the parish, living at what is now Little Badcocks. In the body of his will he leaves the Guildhouse jointly with other property, but he apparently changed his mind just before his death because a codicil shows that he sold it to "Robert Parker and John Grene tenants of the manor". How Hewer obtained the property is not certainly known, but the house was nearly opposite his and its land must have been a convenient addition. Ever afterwards Guildhouse possessed only three acres of its own.

Of John Grene little is discoverable, although a John Grene of Great Birch appears as a juror in 1588, and two births of sons of a John Grene are also recorded in Easthorpe — James in 1591 and John in 1598. Nothing else is known. Robert Parker and Ann Parker both died in 1581; Robert must have been nearly eighty years of age.

Just what happened to the Guildhouse after Robert's death is unclear. Perhaps the Grenes lived there, because the Parkers suffered some sort of decline. The next reference to the Parkers is in the will of Robert Ham (1604), resident at Hunts next door. He refers to a Richard Parker occupying but not owning a "cottage builded in garden" which Ham left to Alice Cable then Henry her son. This may have been the now demolished cottages behind the No Name alongside Well Lane, or it may have been "July House Garden" at the first bend of the same lane, but there are other possibilities almost equally plausible. Wherever the cottage was, the Parkers continued in the parish, five children being born to this Richard between 1611 and 1620. In 1624 occurred the marriage of a Jane Parker, otherwise unknown, to William Nelson. No Parker appears in the 1636 Ship Money return, but a Richard Parker occurs in the Hearth Taxes of 1662 and 1672. Children were born to this Richard in the 1670s, but no subsequent record occurs. The family must thus be presumed to have died out or to have departed the parish during the poorly recorded years of the rector Obadiah Paul. After their departure the land they farmed, probably rented and never of much extent, was absorbed into that farmed by the Chattertons of

Three Village houses, past and present

Joyes and Little Badcocks. Throughout all this time their connection appears to have been with the "cottage" as none is traceable to the Guildhouse.

After Robert Parker, therefore, the Grenes are the most likely possessors, but there is no other certain record till 1619. In that year William Cooke was resident. He may perhaps have been the son of the Robert Cooke who is shown as "surveyor of highways" as early as 1602 and again in 1611; a servant of the same Robert Cooke was buried in 1612. William Cooke was succeeded by Edward Cooke, who died in 1630, and he was in turn succeeded by another Edward who died ten or twelve years later.

Susannah Cooke, daughter of Edward, then held the property. She married Isaac Campion, and they both lived at the Guildhouse until Isaac's death in 1663, whereafter Susannah lived on there alone. She took it into her head to become a regular attender at the Manor court, and indeed at this time she was almost the only one who did attend. It must be because of this that when in her old age in 1703 she at last sold out, the manorial records give an astonishingly full and formal record of the transaction. It would be interesting to know whether this was at her insistence or in her honour.

The purchaser was William Miles, a wealthy butcher of Messing, the same who bought Winterfloods in 1733. Whether he ever occupied the Guildhouse is unknown but it hardly seems likely; if not, then the property must have been labourers' cottages as it was certainly not a farm and there are no wealthy parishioners whose dwellings are uncertain at the time. William Miles died in 1737, and in the same year the Guildhouse was burned down. Whether there was any connection between the two events is unknown, but if he did live there it would be probable that there was.

The manorial court, perhaps still remembering Susannah, certainly took the loss to heart in a way unusual at the time. In 1738 and 1741 it attempted to levy a regular annual fine upon Edward Miles, William's son and heir, until he rebuilt the Guildhouse, but this he certainly never did. The manor court appears at length to have accepted that this fine was unenforceable and the matter lapsed. Thereafter the descent of the land upon which the house stood is of no particular interest. It passed with the rest of Miles property to the de Hornes, (see Winterfloods), although the manorial records continue to record it optimistically as a separate unit.

Chapter Seven
DEMOLISHED OR DECAYED FARMS AND COTTAGES

Hazells
Hazells Farm lay right on the border of the parish, reached by a track from Scottie leading towards Messing. This track still exists as a public footpath. The house seems to have been demolished in the 1880s, its well being remembered by farm labourers alive sixty years later as having continued in existence after the house had gone. Fruit trees in the hedgebanks also gave visible clues to the site till recent years.

Hazells was part of the manor of Bourchiers Hall, Messing, and its name is derived from fifteenth and sixteenth century farmers of the land. A 1422 Compotus mentions Robert Hasille as holding Olives and Doves, land later certainly part of Hazells and possibly bearing its earlier name. John Hasille was witness to a will in 1573, so may either have inhabited or owned the house, but there is a more continuous Easthorpe connection with the family of John Tiler or Tyler of Feering, who leased it from Christopher Chibborne of Bourchiers Hall before purchasing it in the 1590s. A John Tyall of Colchester, draper, dying in 1500, left a tenement in Easthorpe to be sold, while a Richard Tiler is mentioned in the Easthorpe Lay Subsidy of 1524 and is doubtless the same Richard whose will of 1531 leaves all to his son John; he may be the John Tyler who witnessed the receipt of money in Marks Tey in about 1550. Alice, Richard Tiler's wife, died in that same year of 1531, and she thought of her son Christopher as well as John. Christopher received a brass pot with a patch on the side, a coverlet, a sheet, a blanket, two plates and a pewter dish. John received a little brass pot, a little kettle, some bedding and all the "linen gear".

Alice's will also mentions her father, Thomas Anwyke, and her will is witnessed by her brother, William Anwyke. An Anwyke's Meadow is mentioned in the Hazells area in 1520, and it may therefore be that the Anwykes were there before or at the same time as the Tilers. In 1489-90, in the Oath Book of Colchester, occurs a general acquittance by Letitia Grewe, widow of John Grewe of Colchester, to Richard Anwyke of Marks Tey and Thomas Anwyke of Easthorpe. The same source gives an indication of even earlier ownership. The lane, now the footpath, between Scotties and Hazells is shown on a map of 1625 as Suttons Lane, and a Thomas Sutton, glover, born at Easthorpe, became a burgess of Colchester in 1478-9. If, as seems probable, the Easthorpe home of Thomas Sutton was Hazells or some part of it then a reference in the Feet of Fines as early as 1296 may refer to his family's purchase of the property. In that year Thomas de Sutton and Phillipa his wife purchased an unknown number of acres of land in Easthorpe from Richard de Mershton and Cecily his wife. This is the earliest nearly continuous descent of property in the parish, other than manorial descent, that can be surmised with any degree of probability. Whether these de Suttons had any relationship to the John de Sutton who was lord of the manor of Stoke by Nayland in the early part of the fourteenth century is not clear, but he it was who (no doubt as a trustee) granted the manor of Little Birch to Ralph de Tendring. There is also an isolated and later reference to a Robert Sutton who was buried at Easthorpe in 1611 but whether or not he had any connection with the old Sutton property is not known.

Another early reference to land later farmed with, or partly with, Hazells is that

Demolished or decayed farms and cottages

eighty acres of land in Messing and Easthorpe purchased by Robert de Naillynghurst, Clerk, in 1364 and held of John Bourchier. The descent of Bourchiers Hall manor itself is quite clear. Prior to Chibborne it was held briefly by Thomas Diggs of London and before him by the Daniels who had in their turn inherited through marriage with the Baynards. John Daniel senior held Skynns, near Hazells, before his death in 1556, and John Daniel the younger's name appears in various deals relating to land adjacent or near to Hazells before his sale of the manor itself in 1582. At his death in 1584 he was of Wetherden, Suffolk, late of Messing, and is described as the eldest son of Edmund Daniel of Acton Place, also in Suffolk. His wife Alice was daughter of Sir Henry Tyrell.

Chibborne also owned Salmons, a holding of thirty acres adjoining Hazells but in Messing parish (see Scotties), selling it to John Miller the elder and the younger in 1603 or 1604. John Tiler bought this in 1605 for the substantial sum of £80, so turning Hazells into an important farm of some size. His death occurred only two years later, and his will not surprisingly shows him to have been quite a wealthy man by comparison with other local inhabitants. He was certainly living at Hazells at the time of his death. His nephew, another John Tiler, inherited and may have also lived in the house, but when he died it passed to yet a third John Tiler who was living at Brightlingsea, and he quickly sold it to John Conyers of Peldon. Who inhabited Hazells at this stage is not known, but in 1623 the occupier was certainly William Ham and he continued to reside for several years. His time at Hazells cannot have been very happy, because his son William died in 1626 and his daughter Mary in 1629, just before one of his servants.

At this period it is very difficult to say just what constituted "Hazells Farm". Tiny pieces of surrounding land were sold or exchanged and farmed as part of Hazells from time to time, but the general impression is that it began to decline in importance. A series of mortgages and part sales by Conyers and Tiler eventually made John Furley, a linen draper at Colchester, owner in 1635. John Furley was of the parish of St. Runwalds, and as churchwarden was taken to task at the visitation in 1633 for its deplorable condition. He was one of the Puritan leaders of Colchester and was mayor in 1638 and again in 1650. One of the part holders of a mortgage still persisting in Furley's time was Ann Smith, wife of Robert Smith of Kelvedon, the same who set up the Easthorpe charity (see Minor Holdings — Land of Kelvedon Poor).

From the Furley family Hazells gradually passed, again by a long series of successive mortgages, to the Luckyns of Messing. By 1706 they can be said to have owned the major part of it, although as late as 1722 a John Turner of Limehouse still owned a significant amount of the land. Indeed, he actually increased his holding in 1727 when he took over the last vestige of the Furley interest. Nevertheless, the Luckyns continued to consolidate their holding and it descended in the nineteenth century through the Luckyn inheritance to the Earl of Verulam.

The 1637 terrier, made in John Furley's time, states that "the farm called Hazells, a house, other buildings and orchard, with 40 acres of land is wholly in Easthorpe", and certainly at the time of the Civil War it seems to have become stabilised as a small farm. The occupiers at this time were probably the Quaker family of Root, wiped out by a series of deaths in the 1670s. The last of the family, Widow Root, who died in 1677, was certainly one of the five nonconformists reported in the parish (as against 52 conformists) in the previous year. Around 1680-90, when its occupier was John Hurst, it was still farmed as an independent unit and appears to have enjoyed a renewed

Demolished or decayed farms and cottages

prosperity. By the turn of the century it had declined once more and the occupier wa John Hales or Hailes. The Furleys were Quakers and leased to the brethren, bu because as a Quaker Hales refused to pay tithes, his farm was assessed. In 1706 he said to have had:-

    2 acres grey pease
    2 acres wheat
    5 acres clover hay
    fruit and garden stuff
    5 cows and 5 calves
    a sow and ten pigs

These tithes were rented by Isaac Crooke, and it was at his suit that a court cas was brought in 1707.

In 1704 is recorded the burial of "Sarah Birch, spinster, at John Hales' house in th parish", an unusually full entry which may be intended to allude to her also being wel known as a Quaker. There is evidence that John Hales himself was an obdurate mar Eventually he lost the farm and his will of 1730 describes him as a "gardener c Colchester, late of Easthorpe". He left only "some small effects in my own hands an some more effects detained unjustly, for the recovery of which I have exhibited my bi in chancery with some hope of success". This legal reference, however, cannc identify him with the John Hales of the Inner Temple who was involved in financia transactions with Francis Butler of Grays Inn regarding Bockingham Hall and Flispe Butler was a Catholic.

Hales (or Hails) seems to have been dispossessed by stages. Even by 1710 part c his land was in the occupation of William Blowers, presumably a relation of Joh Blowers of Winterfloods, but John Hales was still hanging on to the house in 1712 sinc an "apprentice" of his, William French, is recorded to have been buried in that yea After him it is difficult to discover what, if anything, still constituted Hazells Farm; seems to have been farmed with Scotties. Ambrose Walford, from a Messing famil certainly was there in 1721, but he died in 1724. After his death Hazells was for son time farmed by the Blowers from Winterfloods again, but it is uncertain who lived the house. Apparently in 1746, however, and certainly in 1760, the tenant was certain John Hicks and Hazells briefly became once more an independent entit Strangely enough, Hicks farmed it with a tenement which bore his name (see Minc Holdings), but which had had that name for at least a hundred and fifty years before h time. The cottage on that site is first mentioned during his tenancy and it is quite like that he built it. Hellens, mentioned in the final chapter, is a similar and almo contemporary case of coincidency of name.

In 1779 the Eleys took over the lease in order to farm the land with Scotties, an Hazells has continued as part of that farm ever since. The house at once descended the status of a cottage. In 1835 it was described as "a cottage tenement suitable fo labourers". The eventual demolition of Hazells presumably followed the failure of th Eley line at Scotties which thereby itself became a subsidiary tenancy. Hazells remembered locally as Gants, after its last occupiers. The family of Gant we established there before 1800, though sometimes sharing it with one or two other 'let notably the Springetts.

Demolished or decayed farms and cottages

Winnings

Winnings has been demolished for about two hundred years. Its site was until recently marked by a barn which stood back from the road not far from Scotties Lane and a little nearer the A12, but this barn too has now been pulled down. The evocative name of Winnings is not the only interesting thing about this long-lost dwelling and its history is of some importance.

Winnings is first mentioned by name in the will of John Wright in 1573. He left it after the death of his wife Joan to his son John "with the cottage I have set up separated by a ditch from my said house and land". Wright was not rich, but a typical small farmer of the time, and felt obliged to be precise about the bequest of his "new hosen" and such goods as his "cart and tumbril, harrow, and the harness thereunto belonging". To him these clearly represented the keys to a livelihood.

John Wright senior's own father was another John who died in 1544, but he leased Cawens (Canfields) and it is uncertain whether he too lived at Winnings, though there seems to have been a connection. His wife is likely to have been the "Wright's wife" left a small sum by her father, John Ardleigh of Flispes, in 1532; John Wright himself witnessed this will.

Not only does Winnings adjoin Flispes but it looks on the map as though it may originally have been created from a part of it, although there is no evidence that Flispes was ever of sufficient size for this to have been the case. As Flispes was linked with Bockingham Hall, furthermore, not much support is given to this possibility by Winnings' alternative name of Garlands. The name Garlands is exceedingly common in the neighbourhood and can in most cases be traced with certainty to the Gernons, once of Birch Castle and also lords of the manor of Easthorpe. In the district there are several instances where the name has attached to lands originally pertaining to the Gernons themselves or to the manor of Great Birch, but subsequently to that of Easthorpe.

The earliest recorded owner of "Winnings els. Garlands", as it was known, is surprisingly enough John Kingston, the rector of Easthorpe who died in 1557 and was thus owner in the time of the second John Wright. Kingston left the property to his brother Bernard on a condition so interesting that it must be given in full. Bernard was to pay to the next parson and to his successors for ever "one yearly rent or annuity of seven shillings and two pennies of lawful money of England for the finding and maintaining of one obit . . . The forme and sums spent are to be for the divine celebration of placebo and dirige, nine lessons with commendations 2d; for mass 4d; for the waste of tapers burning on the hearse 2d; the offering of frankincense to be made by the then tenant of Garlands 1d; for the recitation of the name of John Kingston on the bederoll 4d; the sexton for ringing 2d; to him for ordering of the hearse 1d, and to him for helping the priest at mass 2d. And to be given and disposed in bread to the poor people then being present at the mass 5/- and to wax to burn before the sepulchre in the same church 8d. Which obits I will to be disposed and said yearly if the laws of this realm will permit the same. And if it fortune that the law will not so permit I will the same money to be given to the poor of the same parish yearly . . .".

Kingston clearly expected, and rightly, that Mary's death would end the Catholic allegiance of which he was so prominent a local supporter. The bequest accordingly reverted to a charity, as he had proposed, and appears to have been paid yearly as

73

Demolished or decayed farms and cottages

directed. The property must have been sold by Bernard Kingston to the second Joh[n] Wright, who certainly owned it, and sold again by John Wright the third to Stephe[n] Beaumont, rector from 1579. From him it was purchased by John Binder in or abo[ut] the year 1590, but in 1600 Beaumont commenced a lawsuit against Binder for no[n] payment of the charity which it must be presumed he himself had always paid. Bind[er] seems to have been a difficult and litigious man, as his name is frequent in sm[all] lawsuits, and in fact he died the following year — but not before judgment had be[en] given.

A special chancery court, empowered to hear charity cases, sat at the 'Lyon' [at] Kelvedon. The Bishop Suffragan of Colchester, William Ayloff of Braxted, Ral[ph] Wiseman, and Christopher Chibborne of Messing, were appointed to the commissio[n]. Binder claimed that he need not pay because "the charity was absolutely bound [to] superstitious uses", but the puritan rector must have denied that! The judges we[re] quite clear that the charity should be paid, and empowered the rector to distrain upo[n] the owners if eight days in arrears for 1st November (All Saints Day) payment. Th[e] judgment affected not only John Binder, who farmed the land, but also the wido[w] Owen who occupied the "cottage with a rood, parcel of Garnons". The widow is a litt[le] mysterious. John Owen had four children, one dying in infancy, before the death of h[is] wife in 1593; she, presumably, was the Christina Owen who appealed to the courts [to] restrict Robert Wordsworth of Little Birch, because she was afraid he would beat or k[ill] her. It must be supposed that John remarried and then he himself died, for all exce[pt] the 'widow' thereafter disappear from the records. The widow herself may have fou[nd] the Winnings judgment onerous, for she married Richard Carder in 1602.

Thereafter the charity was apparently paid once more because there surviv[e] receipts for six years rent from Mr. Porter (of Badcocks), in 1707 and again for £3 12s [in] 1717 — ten years payment. In 1753 John Halls, rector, received of Mr. Buxton £3 10½d, "which together with £2 17s 8d before received pays up to December las[t]". Anna Porter had married Isaac Buxton of Messing, as related under Peacocks. There [is] no further record, and it must be presumed that the charity thereafter lapsed.

By Binder's will in 1601 the Winnings property descended to "John Stonard th[e] son of John Stonard late of Wakes Colne husbandman". This is likely to have been o[ne] of the John Stonards referred to under Canfields. The property is stated to have been seven acres, about the usual size of ancient holdings in the parish. "Old Stonnard" di[ed] in 1639, although two years earlier Winnings was already called "late Stonnards".

The next certain record of the property is its sale by William Ford of Kelvedon [to] Robert Townsend of Coggeshall exactly fifty years later. Another William For[d], possibly his father and a previous owner, was buried at Easthorpe in 1667, and tw[o] years earlier Elizabeth, wife of this William, gave birth to a daughter. An Alice Fo[rd] was buried in 1668. Earlier still, in 1655, is recorded the death of another "Elizabet[h] wife of William Ford". It is therefore quite possible that the property passed direct[ly] from the Stonnards to the Fords. After the William Ford who died in 1667, however, h[is] family do not appear to have continued in residence. In 1689 the occupier is stated [to] have been Thomas Bacon, presumably he whose name appears, for example, in th[e] Hearth Tax of 1672. There are also other parish records of this Thomas and his wi[fe] Elizabeth, the earliest in 1666; there is an isolated earlier record of the marriage of a[n] Elizabeth Bacon in 1636, so they were perhaps not new to the parish.

Demolished or decayed farms and cottages

Thomas Bacon died in 1692, Thomas Porter of Badcocks and the rector of Great Birch both witnessing his will. Thomas Porter most probably purchased the property from Townsend, but was described as occupier as early as 1685, so Bacon may have been a sub-tenant. Thomas Bacon's son, John, kept on the little farm, but his mother Elizabeth died two years later; Obadiah Paul, rector of Easthorpe, was witness to her will. Like her husband, she left her son Thomas and daughter Elizabeth money to be paid some years later, when it could be squeezed out of the small estate. Like him, too, she is described as "of Copford", though it is not clear why. Elizabeth's will implies that John was expected to keep on the lease, but later tenants are uncertain; perhaps like so many of the smaller farms in the parish at this time it was deemed unviable and ceased its independent existence.

As with Peacocks and other small property nearby, the ownership of Winnings descended through Anna, the Porter heiress, to her niece Anna, wife of David Crumpton. She inherited in 1767 and in this year the property was once again separately leased, this time to Benjamin Ladham of Copford. After his death in 1788 his wife Elizabeth continued the lease for a few more years. Thereafter the occupier was for some time a Samuel Bright, while the ownership had on Crumpton's death passed to Samuel Sparrow of Kelvedon. By 1801 Samuel Sparrow was apparently trying to farm Winnings, Filcocks and St. Johns Garden himself, but soon was succeeded in this endeavour by James Polley.

Some part of Sparrow's combined property was sold to A. Johnson before his death in 1820, apparently in settlement of a mortgage, and all of it, including what had once been Winnings, was by various stages gradually absorbed into the Badcocks farm. At what time the house and the little cottage which once stood beside it were demolished is uncertain, but they had certainly disappeared by 1840 and the circumstances make it likely that they had gone half a century earlier.

Flispes

Flispes

Flispes still stands near Easthorpe Green, once Fouchers, but it is at present a sad sight with its fine and almost unaltered late sixteenth century frame derelict and open to the weather. It is to be restored (almost too late) in 1989. Its presence so close to another one-time farmhouse is unexpected, but Flispes was an isolated outpost of the manor of Bockingham Hall, so its origin may be a pre-conquest land transaction of which all

Demolished or decayed farms and cottages

trace has long been lost: Bockingham Hall manor is often stated (though without much solid evidence) to have been of some importance in Saxon times.

The name Flispes derives from the family of Flisp, known in the parish during the fourteenth and fifteenth centuries. The will of a Richard Flisp of Easthorpe who died in 1419 has survived, and it must have been a close relation who is recorded as of the same name and parish when becoming burgess of Colchester in 1392. Stephen Flisp perhaps this earlier Richard's son, was a prominent burgess in and around 1400 Flispes Farm at this time formed a part of the estate of the Tey family, to whom it had descended from the Gernons. It remained with them until sold to Katherine Audeley of Berechurch along with Badcocks in 1585.

It can be claimed as probable that an unusually early reference to an Easthorpe land transaction alludes to Flispes, because Flispes was the only land of Bockingham Hall Manor in Easthorpe. In the Feet of Fines of 1218 Adam de la Gare was cited as demandant at an assize of mort d'ancestre. William, son of Adam of Easthorpe and of Cil'es his wife, held six acres of land with appurtenances — the normal local size of holding. The tenant quitclaimed to the demandant who was to hold this land of Roger de Bottingham rendering "18d and the ward of Dover 1d and 1d for scutage of 20s for all services". The price was 20s.

At some time during the fifteenth century the Flisp family died out or perhaps migrated permanently to Colchester, and the family of Ardleigh later became established in their place. Their name is frequent in the district, occurring for example in Layer at an early date, but it sounds as though the family were originally from Ardleigh near Colchester. A John Ardleigh of Great Birch was made Burgess of Colchester in 1485, and he may have been related to the John Ardleigh of Flispes whose death occurred in 1532 and whose will has survived. Although this will shares Ardleigh's property equally amongst his sons he desired in respect of the lease that "one shall buy another's part to keep it in the name of Ardleigh". Some such arrangement may indeed have been made, because Nicholas and William Ardleigh successively occupied the farm after him. His son John had moved out of the parish and is probably the John of Aldham whose memory was commemorated by a light in Marks Tey church in 1552.

After the Ardleighs came Peter Spilman, certainly the occupier in 1576, but of him nothing else is known. His tenure was presumably short, because the next certain event is the death of the tenant William Ettene or Eatney, which occurred in 1592. Eatneys were known in the parish before their occupancy of Flispes, and a Richard Eatney, son of John and Anne, was baptised as early as 1572. From William Eatney's will it is apparent that the farm was still a small one at this date because he felt necessary to stage his various bequests over several years in order not to damage its viability. As for immediate bequests, Eatney refers to a double table, seven silver spoons and four ewe sheep.

Elizabeth Eatney, William's wife, was responsible for the bequests and kept on the farm until her own death in 1611. She was apparently assisted by at least two of her sons, but after 1611 they quickly removed to Birch. As early as 1613 William, the eldest, signed a recognisance for John Browne, also of Birch, for keeping an unlicensed alehouse. In 1616 he was in trouble together with a miller and the miller's wife (probably of Little Birch Mill), being admonished to keep the peace towards Richard Potter, blacksmith at Heckfordbridge Smithy. Other Birch records of Eatneys occur

Demolished or decayed farms and cottages

until 1636, when Stephen Eatney was still living in the parish and when William, now of Baddow, sold a small tenement.

The abrupt departure of the Eatneys from Easthorpe came about because when their mother died, Katherine Audeley, already mentioned under Badcocks, at once took the opportunity of leasing Flispes to her servant, Anthony Ashe, who was already farming land called Rosses at Layer de la Haye. How long he held Flispes is not known, but it may be significant that after his time it seems not to have been an independent unit. Its decline is perhaps evidenced by the lack of alteration to the fabric. As for the ownership, it passed from the heirs of Katherine Audeley after her death in 1641 to the family of Shave, the same who became tenants of Little Badcocks. The Shaves themselves declined in prosperity and after the Civil War Flispes appears, rather surprisingly, in the hands of Francis Butler of Bockingham Hall, taking its ownership back to where it started. A long and tedious series of mortgages took place around this time and Flispes eventually went to Nat Piggott, a papist (as was Butler) in payment of a debt. Piggott died in 1717 and in 1727 the property went to Charles Gray, purchaser of so much other property in the district at this time: a few further details are given under Bockingham Hall in the final chapter.

Some seventeenth century tenants are known, but the list is probably incomplete. One was Abraham Freeman, who was married in 1600 so may either have succeeded Elizabeth Eatney on sub-lease from Ashe or else succeeded Ashe himself. This Abraham Freeman was no doubt the minor yeoman who owned a number of small properties in Birch and Peldon and died an old man in 1659, his grandson succeeding. He may well have lived at Flispes in his earlier years, but that cannot be certainly proved. The tenant around the time of the Civil War was Thomas King, but of him little is known but his name.

The most important later tenants were the family of Phillips, but for most if not all of that time they were also tenants and indeed residents of Little Birch Holt. Flispes was probably inhabited by various members of this family from the middle of the century onwards, but it is uncertain exactly which ones. The Hearth Tax returns, for example, give John Phillips' name for both Little Birch Holt and Flispes. The family came from Birch and the will of a John Phillips who died there in 1638 is extant. He appears to be the John Phillips, grocer, who with the puritan John Argent was granted the manor of Copford Hall but sold it to the Mountjoys in 1610. It was either his son or more probably his grandson who became prominent at Easthorpe, where the first mention of the name occurs in 1653; in this year John Phillips of Easthorpe (and perhaps of Flispes), son of John Phillips of Birch, married Elizabeth Rand, daughter of Richard Rand of the Hall. It is also interesting that Elizabeth, sister of John Phillips, married Thomas Shave, whose connection with Flispes was mentioned earlier.

John Phillips and his wife, another Elizabeth, had at least four children in the late 1650s and 1660s, but after the birth of Susannah in 1667 Elizabeth must have died because John is recorded as marrying Sarah Theobald the following year. He was sufficiently prosperous for his daughter Elizabeth to marry into the wealthy Milbanks family in 1685, but in the same year the register records the birth of a daughter, yet another Elizabeth, to "Gilbert and Elizabeth Phillips", so perhaps the marriage with Gilbert Milbanks was insisted upon: this Gilbert Milbanks was the tenant of Shemmings in Birch, or perhaps his son. Nothing else of relevance to Flispes is recorded until John Phillips himself died in 1704, closely followed by his daughter Susannah, wife of John

Demolished or decayed farms and cottages

Golding of Kelvedon. Susannah's little boy John, described in the register as "grandso of widow Phillips", died in 1708, and before her own death in 1716 the widow sa another grandson, John Phillips, buried in 1712. It must have been a sad househol John Phillips the second of Little Birch Holt died in 1721.

One of the daughters of John Phillips the elder was called Ann, and she marrie Thomas Theobald or Tibbald. That family had been established at Birch for man years, and also had connections with a number of farms in Easthorpe, notably Scottie Old Widow Phillips resided at Flispes towards the end of her life, so before 1716 th Tibbalds rented the land from year to year, but after her death in that year there was more continuous arrangement. They may have begun as under-tenants of Joh Phillips the second, as one deed states that such did exist. Thomas Tibbald w: succeeded by his son, another Thomas, whose death did not occur till 1769. Flispes w: never again farmed as a separate unit but was united with Fouchers: possibly appeared an anachronism even before Thomas's death, for his will shows that he w by no means prosperous.

Flispes thereupon became a farm cottage, and the names of many of its tenants a known. Perhaps the longest lived were a couple named Mole, a name still recalled the parish, who inhabited it for most of the nineteenth century and died at a great ag Mrs. Mole, aged 75 in 1858, was that year the victim of a bizarre incident, beir accused of putting spells on the livestock of the Braziers — by, for example, causir one of their pigs to climb a cherry tree and eat the fruit. Although there were sever family units called Brazier in the village at that time the censuses of 1851 and 18(contain no record of the accuser, Emma Brazier, aged 22 at the time of the incident. is probable, however, that she lived in Easthorpe Green Cottage, close by, which w. certainly occupied by Braziers at the time. The rector, George Bowles, consider Emma to be deranged, and the Braziers called in the famous "Cunning Murrel himself to effect a cure. A crowd gathered and the rector had to guard the cotta; door. At this juncture Emma threatened the life of Mrs. Mole and was eventua detained by the police, who also had to disperse the crowd. Following this incident was rumoured that the rector was a believer in witchcraft, and he felt obliged to wri letters to the newspapers denying it.

Joyes

Joyes was a long, low cottage of a type once common in the area but now rare. It sto beside the Roman Road at the south eastern corner of the rectory grounds and was n demolished until recent times. The name presumably derives from the family of Sim Joye and John Joye mentioned in an Easthorpe deed of 1418. Earlier still, in 1265 Peter Joye is mentioned as one of the two keepers of the manor of Easthorpe for t king during the temporary deprivation of Sir Ralph Gernon. Later on, in 1447, Nicholas Joye born at Easthorpe was made a burgess of Colchester, so it may be th the Joyes prospered and moved away in the same way as did apparently so many oth late mediaeval families of Easthorpe.

Joyes is recorded in 1555 as having been sold by Thomas Hewer (of Fennes, nc Little Badcocks) to Robert Kidd for £16 in gold and £4 in silver. This newly independe existence can hardly have been a prosperous one, however, as its fields were sc away at various times and by 1650 even the house was with Little Badcocks again. such it passed with Little Badcocks through all subsequent ownerships, though it w for the most part tenanted as a separate small farm until the early eighteenth centu

Demolished or decayed farms and cottages

Joyes (from old Photograph)

Its occupiers cannot always be proved with certainty, but the names of many of those who farmed pieces of land at this end of the parish on the Copford border are known from the records and amongst them are some who can be positively identified as holding Joyes. In particular, the families of Chatterton and Glascock appear to have lived there at various times during the seventeenth and eighteenth centuries. The Chattertons are mentioned from about 1630 to 1660, but in this year Robert Chatterton died aged only 22, and thereafter they do not appear again until early in the next century. It is not certain that during this second period they came back to live at Joyes, because some of their land was in Little Birch and Copford, but it is highly probable because they appear in the parish records and their wills are "of Easthorpe". Francis Chatterton the elder, who died in 1706, was the younger of the sons of John Chatterton and was born in 1640. Joanna Chatterton, his widow, was buried in 1718.

The family of Glascock is similarly traceable in the parish records and elsewhere. Francis Glascock took over from the Chattertons in 1660. His first wife Mary died in that year, but he married a second of the same name, presumably "the widow Glascock" who died in 1706. Francis himself died soon after 1680, after which Daniel Phillibrowne farmed the land, whether or not the widow continued to live on at Joyes. The Glascocks had at least six children, but only Susannah appears to have survived. In 1712 she too died, with the strange addition in the register "a friend of Daniel Hallbread", he being most probably a wealthy tenant of the Hall who himself died two years later.

Our only knowledge of the standard of life at Joyes at the time is derived from the wills of the Chattertons, from which it appears that that standard was not very high. Francis Chatterton made his will in 1701, leaving "the bed we lie on" to his wife and £6 a year to be paid by his son Daniel "if she chooses to live with him". William Turner, his son-in-law, was also a small beneficiary. Francis died in 1706 and Daniel must have had a hard struggle till his own death in 1714. Just before this he received a gift of £20 from Lydia Wade of Little Badcocks, who may have been a Chatterton herself, but for Daniel it was too late. His will divided his interest in the property, implying that it was no longer a worthwhile unit. The burial of Daniel's mother, Joanna, is recorded in 1718 but the Chattertons otherwise disappear from the annals. Their departure marked the

Demolished or decayed farms and cottages

end of Joyes as an independent holding and it was ever after no more than a farm cottage of Little Badcocks.

Peacocks

Just before the drive to Badcocks on the way out of the village, and on the same side of the road, a change in the hedge marks the site of Peacocks. Although this was an ancient holding not much is discoverable of its earlier years of independence. Nor can much more be said of its long subsequent subordination to Badcocks; no doubt the names of those who inhabited it are amongst the many names in the parish register whose dwelling is now untraceable.

The name Peacock, Pecok or Paycocke is widely known in the district, particularly along the Essex/Suffolk border, and it often occurs in the records of Colchester itself. Mentions in the thirteenth and fourteenth centuries are frequent. The best known memorial to the family today is, of course, the spectacular house in Coggeshall still known as Paycocks. Thomas was a popular first name with the Coggeshall branch of the family, and it is just possible that there may be a connection with the only Easthorpe reference to the name, the Thomas Pecok who witnessed the will of William Vesye in 1524. It is no doubt from this Thomas Pecok or some relation that the Easthorpe property was so called.

No further record of the house appears until Peacocks is mentioned as owned and occupied by the Turner family of Badcocks and of Fouchers. Their ownership must date from the early years of the seventeenth century and the dwelling was presumably used as labourers' cottages. In 1675, however, it was purchased by John Hurst and seems for a few years to have enjoyed a more independent existence, but in 1684 it was sold again to John Furley, owner of Hazells, and any pieces of land it may have acquired were merged once more into other holdings.

About ten years later it was sold to Thomas Porter. The significance of this sale is uncertain; Badcocks was tenanted by Porters at the time but they were John Porters even though a Thomas was born to them in 1705. The main Porter line, who often called themselves Thomas, were from Messing, and Peacocks was certainly in the hands of a Thomas Porter of Messing when he died in 1730 — but it does appear that this was Thomas son of John. Isaac Buxton, also of Messing, thereupon inherited through his marriage to the Porter heiress, Thomas's elder sister Anna. There was another sister, Mary, married to Jonathan Ardlie and again of Messing, but Isaac Buxton bought out her interest in the Easthorpe properties. The connection of the Buxtons and Porters is worth mentioning. Their common interest was in nonconformity, and when in 1710 a new meeting house, the Coggeshall Independent Chapel, was built, the names mentioned in deeds include those of Isaac Buxton of Great Coggeshall, clothier, Thomas Porter senior of Messing, gentleman, and Thomas Porter Junior of Easthorpe, yeoman. Isaac Buxton became a trustee. Thomas Porter of Inworth, Gent., was appointed a new trustee in 1727.

The history of the Buxtons is traceable but has no relevance to Easthorpe until the time of Thomas Buxton (1643-1713), so militant a noncomformist that he narrowly escaped prison. An Isaac was his only child, and was described by one who knew him in glowing terms: "he joined to a fine person a very keen and active temper in his business of clothier" and was "jealous in his noncomformity". He is recorded as dying of the palsy in his 60th year (1732). This Isaac had five sons, "all men of sincerity, great honesty and sound sense". The eldest two, Thomas and John, were clothiers, but Isaac

Demolished or decayed farms and cottages

of Messing was a draper and grocer. All were strict nonconformists, and all were buried at Coggeshall.

In addition to Peacocks, Isaac Buxton of Messing also inherited Filcocks, the history of which is described later in this chapter, but for some reason he later split his holding. Peacocks he sold in 1744 to a John Harris, who like John Hurst before him seems to have made the attempt to set up Peacocks as a separate unit with a few acres. It was probably not very successful, because when he died in 1766 his son Joseph promptly sold the property to William May of Badcocks, another nonconformist. Peacocks, together with other small properties in the vicinity, was inevitably attractive to men like May who tenanted large farms which they would never own.

After William May retired to Upminster in 1800 he did not sell Peacocks but retained it until his death in 1813. It thus passed to his son-in-law Joseph Giblin, and continued in his ownership for many years. It was never again more than a farm cottage, but was probably of a higher standard than most others as it was occupied as a single let. Uriah Fisher and his family were the inhabitants for much of the century. Later it became a beerhouse and is still remembered to have been spoken of as such by old farm labourers in the 1920s.

St. Johns Garden

This cottage, long demolished, stood opposite Scotties Lane and was an outlying possession of the Newland Manor of Witham. Its exact frontage is still visible as a cessation in the ditch at this point. Newland was a possession of the Knights Templar and afterwards of the Knights Hospitallers of St. John of Jerusalem until their suppression in 1540. Their holdings were regranted on their refoundation by Queen Mary in 1556 but again lost on their further suppression after her death two years later. The derivation of the name is thus obvious and indicates a long history for this little property. Although no certain record of it can be traced in the surviving records of Newland Manor it must be presumed to have been a gift to the Templars or Hospitallers in mediaeval times.

One possible connection suggests itself. The Order of St. John of Jerusalem was founded in 1148 by Jordan Briset. He not only held land in Witham but also Prested Hall, a Manor to which the site of St. Johns Garden Cottage is very close. The Hospitallers attracted an enormous number of Essex benefactions and a thorough search of its cartulary, now in the British Museum, might yet enable the original gift to be traced.

The position of St. Johns Garden, quite isolated from the rest of the manor, would probably have led to its immediate consolidation with other Easthorpe properties after the final suppression of 1558. There is no trace of its ever having land or being a viable farmstead in its own right, and it may be that it was never more than a farm cottage.

The Porters of Badcocks were in possession of St. Johns Garden from about 1703 when it was sold by John Francis with Filcocks, and like Peacocks and Filcocks it passed in 1730 to Isaac Buxton by inheritance through his wife Anna Porter. Unlike Peacocks, however, it was not sold away, the reason for this apparently being a dispute concerning title. There are several records in the 1730s of a protracted and not easily determinable dispute arising from some earlier land dealings of John Porter. In 1733 Isaac Buxton actually had to surrender the property to a certain Samuel Carter for a while, though he subsequently recovered it. There are references also to a dispute

Demolished or decayed farms and cottages

about the cottage some thirty years previously, when it was "unjustly seized by Hugh Hunt", and it thus seems that the Porters' title can never have been very secure.

St. Johns Garden therefore remained with Buxton, passing in 1766 by inheritance to his niece, married to Daniel Crumpton of Coggeshall. Crumpton held on to one of two small pieces of land which Buxton had accumulated, but promptly sold St. Johns Garden Cottage itself to William May, who had taken over the lease of Badcocks three years before and was no doubt keen to own some property. The reason for Crumpton's prompt sale may have been that St. Johns Garden, like Filcocks, was used by the overseers for the poor of the parish, and therefore he found it of limited value. The appropriation of properties for this purpose is likely to date from the end of the occupancy of Isaac Marriage, shown in the records as tenant of both cottages before William May and certainly gone before 1767.

When William May retired to Upminster in 1800 he sold St. Johns Garden, with Filcocks, to Samuel Sparrow of Kelvedon. In 1815 it was sold again to a more logical possessor, the Rev. Fitzthomas, owner of Badcocks. In 1830, however, the cottage was again purchased by the tenant of Badcocks, this time Thomas Eley. The impression left by the frequent land dealings in the small properties of the parish, of which this is just one example, is of repeated hopes of creating some yeoman holding independent of the large but invariably absentee landowners — but such hopes were always frustrated. In the case of St. Johns Garden, it was destined to be no more than a farm cottage for the rest of its days.

Filcocks
Filcocks, sometimes known as Fellocks, still stands as two much altered cottages not far from the lane to Badcocks and almost opposite the site of Peacocks. The name derives from its original connection with the manor of Felix Hall, Kelvedon, originally Filiols Hall. Sir John de Bohun held this manor at his death in 1433 and it had at that time appurtenances in Easthorpe. There is too an earlier de Sutton connection with this manor, so there may be a connection with land in Easthorpe purchased in 1296 by Thomas de Sutton and Philippa his wife (see Hazells).

During the earliest traceable ownerships Filcocks had just over an acre of land attached, but it may have originally been much more extensive. At the end of the sixteenth century Sir Edward Bullock possessed not only Fouchers but also Nunscroft both in Easthorpe. This cannot have been the adjoining lands of Flispes, but probably was not far away. The suspicion is strengthened by a twelfth century deed whereby the

Filcocks

Demolished or decayed farms and cottages

Filiol family made various gifts to the nunnery of Elstow after ineffective gifts to the nunnery of Wix.

In 1637 and again in 1654 its ownership was with John Emory of Copford — that is, with the owner of Well Cottage. The next certain record is its sale by John Francis to John Porter of Badcocks along with St. Johns Garden, an event which occurred in or soon after 1703; Francis had perhaps been farming both as a small unit. This John Francis is no doubt he whose birth is shown in the parish register as the son of John and Barbara in 1636. John senior died in 1659 and "widow Francis" in 1667. John Francis the second is recorded in the Hearth Taxes and so too, in the registers, are the births of various children to him and his wife Elizabeth. The latest mentions of the family are the burials of a Barbara Francis and a Rachael Francis, daughters of John, in 1703. The likely explanation of this is that he first tenanted then purchased Filcocks, and that his father's holding was St. Johns Garden.

Thereafter the history of Filcocks is exactly the same as St. Johns Garden. Its use was partly as a farm cottage of Badcocks and, again with St. Johns Garden, it was used by the overseers for the poor of the parish during the later eighteenth century. For most of the nineteenth century it was inhabited by the family of Brazier, well known in the parish until recent years.

Minor Holdings

There are many references in the records to small properties of which little can be traced or which seem to have had little or no independent existence for several centuries past. In some cases their sites can be identified with reasonable confidence, but it is not always clear whether there was a dwelling: the term "tenement", in this parish at least, by no means always indicates the presence of a house even when coupled with the phrase "with yards and appurtenances".

Most of the more obscure references are early, few of them persisting beyond the end of the seventeenth century. On the other hand there is one single instance in Easthorpe of a new but late holding under the manor, namely Raymonds. "Thomas Raymond for a cottage 6d", is given as an addendum to the manor rental of 1698 and is not mentioned in the terrier of 1637. This cottage appears to have stood at the end of a short length of track which leaves the second bend in Well Lane about three hundred yards south of the church. Raymonds Meadow, shown as such on the Tithe Map of 1841, preserves the name. The site was low-lying, wet and unhealthy, and only two generations of the family appear to have lived there. Daniel Raymond, or Rayment, who died in 1794 and kept the shop at Hunts (the No Name), was the last of the family recorded in the parish.

Also in the parish was land long known as Spicers. This name certainly refers to the family of Spice, whose arms were at one time in a window of the church. The connection is with the manor descent; Richard Spice married Alice, daughter of co-heiress of Thomas Mandeville, some time after 1400 and assumed his wife's arms. The death of his son Roger is recorded in 1460; he was buried at Black Notley. Roger's son, Clement, died in 1483, and his son held the manor of Motts in Lexden in 1485. An earlier Clement Spice was commoning his beasts in Broomefield near Lexden Hill in 1405, and apparently held the same small manor, but the main branch of the family was from Bocking and, earlier, Rainham.

The land known as Spicers was part of the endowment of Richard Heynes's

Demolished or decayed farms and cottages

chantry in St. Peters, Colchester, founded before 1473; Richard Heynes was born at Layer Marney. Spicers was enfeoffed to John Wingfield, William Tey and Richard Hamond, but on the suppression of the chantry the lands were sold in 1551 by the bailiffs of Colchester "to Robert Leche and others" and are described as "one field, with one acre of meadow, and a garden, containing in the whole, 4 acres — Stretecroft with a lane thereto adjoining, 1 acre ½ — a croft parcel of Spicers, 1 acre ½ — meadow, a moor, called Laneryemarsh, half an acre".

Laneryemarsh and Stretecroft are known names, and they allow Spicers to be plausibly identified with some of the series of small fields just west of the Domsey Brook. A few of these tiny enclosures still survive on the wetter ground, and one still contains a shed as a successor building to a small barn. They have the appearance of separate tenements, almost of garden plots, abandoned through population decline. Spicers, low and marshy, does not look promising land as an entity or separate unit.

Spicers is apparently the "Mr. John Demon's farm" referred to in the most coherent part of the parish boundary description of 1630 which appears in the front of the Register. The other occasional references to Spicers during the hundred years from 1551 are uninformative until 1660, in which year Jonas Damyon, "the unprofitable servant of the lord", left in his will the messuage or tenement called Spicers and Bretts with outhouses, barns, etc., to his son John; at this time it was in the occupation of John Ruffle, doubtless the same shown as having one chimney in the Hearth Tax of 1662. The house may be supposed to have stood adjacent to the barn. John Ruffle died in December of the same year, 1662; he is specifically and unusually mentioned in the village records as "householder", presumably to distinguish him from the Philip Ruffle who is mentioned after 1654. The son of Jonas Damyon, another Jonas, likewise died in the parish in 1662, but his house had three chimneys.

Where in the parish the Damyons themselves lived is difficult to know, though Winterfloods seems most likely. They probably originated from the house of Damyons inside the Marks Tey boundary, in which parish the family are mentioned as occupying land in as early as 1418. Henry Damyon held land in Easthorpe in 1422; earlier still, in 1294, a William Damyon from Marks Tey occurs in the Feet of Fines. No fewer than five of the family are mentioned under that same parish in the Lay Subsidy of 1524, and Moretons is known to have been one of the houses they inhabited at that time. Both the Jonas Damyons, however, were of Easthorpe, and the elder refers in his will to his house containing the "low room called my parlour" as well as to "my colt which I do call Chibb".

In 1741 a map shows the boundary between the lands of Easthorpe Hall and those of Spicers to which it refers as "Mr. John Damonds land". Their ownership of Spicers was thus probably continuous, but they may or may not have resided on it. The last Damyon in the district — also of Easthorpe at the time of his death, but earlier of Rivenhall — was Joseph, who died in 1782. He left three daughters but no sons; one of the girls received his tent bed with appurtenances and a silver tankard. The property known as Damyons was already in several different occupations and was to be sold. Grace "Demmon", of Kelvedon, widow, presumably Joseph's wife and last of the name, was buried at Easthorpe in 1799, aged 77. Of Spicers there is no mention as such in Joseph Damyon's will, though it was very likely among the lands to which he referred. It must have already been consolidated into other holdings, and nothing further is heard of it as a separate entity.

Demolished or decayed farms and cottages

A tenement known as Hicks receives occasional mention, the first in 1625 when it is shown on a map of Hazells Farm as a three acre holding on the Easthorpe village side of Scotties Lane. The name probably derives from a John Hike or Hick mentioned in the Compotus of 1422, but no history of it as a separate holding is discoverable. There is evidence in mortgages and other deeds that it was farmed with Hazells for many years; its history in this connection has already been described. There is no reference to a dwelling before 1746, when it is specifically mentioned that Hicks "has a tenement builded and an orchard". This dwelling survived as a cottage until the present century.

Flanders and Georges, described as a croft with three acres in Easthorpe and Birch, also makes sporadic appearances in the records. 'Flanders' is of uncertain derivation, but 'Georges' probably refers to Robert George (see Badcocks) who owned much land in the area at the end of the sixteenth century. It is also possible that this is the tenement called Salynge referred to in 1576 as lately occupied by John George, deceased. The Georges remained a prominent family in Copford until the middle of the seventeenth century. An unexpectedly late reference to Flanders and Georges occurs in 1763, at which time it was part of the property of Mary Garmond when she was remarried to Matthew Edwards: Mary was the daughter of William Miles, the wealthy Messing butcher mentioned under the Guildhouse and Winterfloods. After this date it was certainly always with Winterfloods, and it seems likely that this had been the case much earlier too. The site of the croft was near Raymonds cottage, amongst low-lying land to the west of Well Lane. The field name "Georges croft" survived there into the nineteenth century.

The only charity relating to Easthorpe other than that of Winnings did not benefit the parish at all. In 1637 Robert Smith left to John Wakering and four others his messuage and lands in Easthorpe, to the end that after his decease the yearly rent from it should be given weekly in bread to the poor of Kelvedon parish every Sunday from 1st November to 1st May. He also made the rather odd provision that after the death of James Smith, his brother, and of his daughter, provided that she died without an heir, the distribution should cease at Kelvedon and commence at Great Horkesley instead. In 1662 an heir was born, or rather an heiress, so the distribution continued at Kelvedon.

A charity report of the 1820s records that the land was rented to Thomas Polley for £12, regularly paid, and that each poor family received a half quartern loaf distributed on Christmas Day and each Sunday thereafter so long as the money lasted. The land itself consisted of five separate pieces, arable and pasture, of about eight acres in all, and these can be precisely identified on old maps of the area and on the tithe map of 1841, being always referred to as the "Poor of Kelvedon Land". They do not form a very convenient holding, being so scattered as to be quite inconsequent, and it would add greatly to our knowledge of the early parish history if the way in which the holding had originally been created could be ascertained. Of the five separate pieces of land, each interesting in itself, four are to the west of the Domsey Brook, one of them being a long and thin piece of suspiciously mediaeval shape known as Street Croft. The fifth is a remarkable L-shaped field which surrounds Little Badcocks to the west and north. In 1637, at the time of the bequest, there was a dwelling, but it seems to have disappeared quite soon afterwards. How Robert Smith himself obtained possession of the land is uncertain, but his wife Ann was part-holder of one of the Hazells mortgages, so the likelihood is that it was by inheritance.

Chapter Eight

SOME OTHER VILLAGE INHABITANTS

Although Easthorpe is only a small village, the writer of its history quickly becomes aware of how very many names in the parish register and other records cannot be certainly ascribed to any particular house or holding. The majority of these, though not all, will have been servants or farm labourers, and indeed many receive only a single reference. Even so their number is impressive and shows how partial is the picture any history can give.

Sessions records are one such source of names of otherwise unknown inhabitants and are the most tantalising because of their reflection of actual incidents which must have caused a stir at the time. For example, John Bundocke of Birch, a butcher, was fined 20s in 1615 for keeping an unlicensed alehouse, despite recognisances being entered into by Edward Stanton of Little Tey, Gent., and the well-known Miles Graye of Colchester, bellfounder. Interestingly enough, the inhabitants of Birch had in the previous year supported his application for a licence to keep an alehouse, even though one already existed on the main road. In 1616 the same Bundocke was accused of killing two calves in Lent with the intention of selling them. In 1621 John Webb of Easthorpe, also a butcher, was cited to give evidence against the same man, who may have been harming his trade. Of this John Webb nothing else is known from the Easthorpe records, but it would be interesting to know whether professional jealousies lay behind the case. Bundocke was still only a butcher at this time, however, because in 1618 the coveted alehouse licence was granted at last to Joshua Eateney (once of Flispes) in his "house against the church" in Great Birch. There may have been some connection between the two families because in 1623 their names were again linked. On this occasion Stephen Eateney, usually of Easthorpe but at that time of Great Birch, had illegally built a cottage without four acres, and John Bundocke, butcher, had lived in it for eleven months.

Unidentifiable wills are a particular source of puzzlement. Some of them are typical 'memorandum' wills of the period, jotted down at the bedside of a dying parishioner or merely related to the rector by someone present at a death. In Easthorpe these are always the work of Kingston or the Beaumonts. Typical examples are those of Edmund Wardner (1601) and Richard Middleton (1625), who gives "the least of his three hutches" to his son-in-law Joseph Tabor and "all his goods beside with the wood in the yard" to his brother-in-law Robert Wade of Messing. One rather casually written Easthorpe will gave trouble. Priscilla Fuller (1640) had it written "by Mr. Browne at the house of William Cox in Coxhall". In 1647 William Cox, a substantial clothier, had to attest to one Mercy Joggins, who contested the provisions, that he remembered this being done. The items Priscilla left were quite unremarkable: her great bible, some bedlinen, various brass objects and her warming pan.

Two wills give particular cause for regret that no more is known of those who made them. One of these is that of Richard Cranfield, churchwarden, and a staunch supporter of the Beaumonts' puritan ideas, at least in his younger days. He was probably born in the village, his father being another Richard and his mother, Mary recorded as buried in 1574. He was a ploughwright by trade, and had six children

Some other village inhabitants

baptised between 1579 and 1594. At his death in 1623 he must have been aged about seventy, and he had recently removed himself, his poultry, his three cows, his brass and his bedding to the house of his son Richard at Tolleshunt Darcy. Whether this did not work out well, or whether he had already made other gifts to Richard is hard to decide, but Richard was given only twelve pence while his other children had gifts of up to three pounds plus various goods. Richard the younger may not have prospered at Tolleshunt or perhaps had no family: his burial at Easthorpe in 1643 is the last record of the Cranfields in the village.

The ploughwright's business went to the youngest Cranfield son, John, presumably when his father left to live with Richard, but he does not seem to have made a success of it. In 1618 he was presented for playing bowls on a Sunday, and in 1624 William Goodall, labourer, and William Clarke, yeoman, were told to keep the peace towards him: by 1636 he was living in Birch. William Clarke was no doubt the same who inhabited Fouchers, and William Goodall one of his employees, perhaps father of John Goodall, the "parish clerk and ancient inhabitant of the parish" who died in 1717; the cause of the quarrel does not appear.

The second particularly interesting will is that of John Lamb, described as a turner, who died in 1559. Although his place of residence in the village is not known his will makes it clear that he traded over a considerable distance. He gives a lengthy list of those to whom he owes money and of those who owe it to him. Cash flow must have been important to the business because the sums of money involved in these transactions seem large in relation to the money and property he actually bequeathed. Amongst the items he lists as supplied but not yet paid for are a large quantity of "pots", also a "wheel" sent to a shoemaker, both these customers being in the Stock/Billericay area. He supplemented his income by farming, it may be presumed, because he leaves to the poor "a seme of the rye in my barn". His cousin, Charles Lamb, was left his best coat, best hose and leather jerkin. He also left money to be paid to his daughters on their marriage, but provided that if his wife were to remarry and her husband "do not use my children well", then his cousin, a harness maker at Hockley, was to take the stock out of their hands.

Before Lamb's time the Lay Subsidy of 1524 provides material for analysis of the relative prosperity of the village and its inhabitants. Unfortunately the two early and important Lay Subsidies of 1319-20 and 1380-1 do not survive for Easthorpe. A few unrelated figures do remain on a damaged page from the earlier of the two, but they are of little use, and the latter is altogether lost for the entire hundred. They leave a sad gap in our knowledge of the mediaeval village.

In 1524 the Subsidy classified its contributors into a number of categories, as follows:

those who had lands to an annual value of £1 or more
those with goods worth £2 or more
those over sixteen years with wages of over £1 per annum
 (in effect a senior living-in servant)
those over sixteen years with earnings of over £1 per annum
 (in effect the more prosperous labourers)

It has been estimated that the land or goods values shown can be considered as approximating to gentry or large farmers at £10 - 50, yeomen at £2 -10, and

Some other village inhabitants

husbandmen/labourers at below that. The poorest people, of course, did not appear at all.

Against this background the divisions in Easthorpe society are interesting. All inhabitants are classified under goods except for two who qualify by wages (the younger Twedes) and Robert Parker who qualifies through 20s earnings. Far and away the richest parishioner is John Hewer at £40. This compares with Thomas Tey, the major local landowner, at £100, and Robert Forster of Birch Hall, lord of the manor, at £66. John Ardleigh of Flispes is in second place for Easthorpe, at £16, a testimony to the earlier importance of that now forgotten farm and exceptional in the area. Next comes William Twede at £8, his two sons Richard and Nicholas both also being in the list at 20s wages each; the Twedes were probably of Badcocks, and are known to have held lands in Lexden as well. John Goodwin at £6 and Nicholas Goodwin at £4 both also had holdings outside the parish, one at least of them being from Hunts (No Name). William Vesye, of the Guildhouse, was rated at £6; this was the year of his death. The rest of the ratings tail off. Richard Tyler, of Hazells, is valued as 60s, and Henry Woodward, possibly of Hoggets, as 40s. The other ancient farms of the parish must be represented by Widow Parker, 40s; John Shelton, 40s; Hugh Roo or Ros, 40s; and John Stegg, 20s. This, then, was the sum total of the 'yeomen' population, and 'prosperous labourers' were hard to find.

Of their predecessors, the mediaeval inhabitants, even less can be said except in those cases where they can be traced to particular houses. The absence of early manorial records, with the sole exception of some fifteenth century estreats included under the manor of Messing Hall, leaves us in almost total ignorance. There are a number of references in Colchester records to former inhabitants who migrated to the borough and became burgesses: two such are William de Easthorpe, taxed as a mercer or draper in 1296 and 1301, and John Spendlove, admitted burgess in 1409. Nothing else is known of either. Also in the borough records are references to a William Davey of Easthorpe and Christine his wife who purchased a messuage there in 1344, and to a sale by John Hurlebat of Easthorpe of 25 acres in Great Birch to Ralph de Tendring. There is, too, a whole series of fourteenth century land transactions in nearby parishes in the name of John of Easthorpe or John Clarke of Easthorpe: if this 'clerke' were the rector it would be John de Hemesby, but there is no evidence that this is so. Again there are references to large landholdings, but they are rarely explicit; such, for example, are references to land in the parish held by Joan Baud (wife of William Baud, whose name survives in Boarded Barns), Walter de Bottingham, William de Esthalle, Joan de Codwill and others. They are not traceable to particular properties and do not add materially to our knowledge.

The parish registers in later times are of course more explicit, but unlike the registers of some other parishes which are fortunate in containing illustrative detail, is rare for them to give more than a name. Occasionally a vagrant wanders off the Great Road to die, as did in 1629 "a vagrant called Evans of Stratford Bow", but that is the most important event normally recorded. Bastards are sometimes mentioned though not frequently: one is instanced in 1716, when there occurred the death of "a unbaptised child of Mary Wade, servant". Some entries have a story behind them which we can now only guess; perhaps, for example, it was Stephen Beaumont, zealous in his early days after the absentee laxness of his predecessor, who was responsible for "Tone and his wife and two children baptised". There are the obvious happy occasions, as in 1807 when Thomas Eley married Mary Polley and Edward Cob

Some other village inhabitants

married her sister Elizabeth on the same day, each witnessing the others' register entries — and there are sad occasions as when in 1801 "William Everett, an infant of two years, drowned in the well".

Where families remained in the parish for some years it is often possible to trace interesting circumstances illustrative of the lives, fortunes and attitudes of the country people of the time. It is worthwhile to record here a few such instances from the mid eighteenth century. There were, inevitably, the very prolific families. To John and Elizabeth Everett, a name well-known in the parish till very recent years, were born Joseph, 1745-9; Jonathan, 1748-52; Joseph, James and Esther 1751, all dying the same year; and Joseph and Esther both born 1753, of whom nothing further is known. To John and Mary Wade were born in 1745 William and Mary, dying the same year; in 1746 another William and Mary; then Elizabeth born in 1748, Thomas in 1749 and James and Mary in 1752.

Both these were labouring families, but in the farmhouses breeding could be just as free and just as subject to mixed fortunes. William Eley, of Hazells, and later Canfields, married Susannah May in 1756. Their children were William, 1759-9, Susannah 1760-97, William, 1763-96, and Ann 1764-4: Ann's birth was the last, her mother dying four days later. William May, of Badcocks, married Sarah Cox of Copford and had five children, none twins, in six years. At Winterfloods Susanna Potter, wife of Richard, gave birth to Richard (1759), John (1762), Sarah (1764), and Charles (1766). At Canfields, Mary, wife of Daniel Gilder, had twins, Mary and Hannah, in 1760, but Hannah died soon after birth. Their only son, Daniel, was born the following year and lived to be old, but the Gilders had only one other child, another Hannah, and she survived no longer than her namesake.

These extracts from the records give an impression of fecundity, but in general this would not be true. Much more common are examples of marriages which apparently yielded only one or two children, and if these or a parent died then the family soon disappears from the records. For instance, at Hoggets Thomas and Martha Garrod or Garrard had only one child, Ann, born in 1761; she survived until 1769, when Thomas died, but Ann and her mother then seem to have given up the lease and moved away. At Well Cottage Samuel and Lucy Christmas had moved from Birch in about 1762, and although their daughter Lucy (born 1765) lived only two years and Ann (1768) only one, their son Samuel, born at Birch, did survive. At the Hall John and Margaret Osborn baptised their last child in 1759, but that boy, called William, was the second of his name to die soon after birth.

There are a few further references around this time to travellers buried at Easthorpe because they died within the parish limits. The most explicit is to "Samuel Cornwell, a poor travelling boy from Hatfield Broad Oak". Whether he died on the short stretch of the Great Road within the parish boundaries, or whether he had turned off it in distress, or whether he was deliberately passing through Easthorpe itself, can now only be a matter of speculation. Today his death, like the others of his kind, is best seen as a reminder that Easthorpe was not a wholly remote parish but was near the great highway from London to East Anglia, and that its affairs must have been affected by this in ways we can now only surmise.

Many other outlines of family histories might be given, but they would be little different from those which occur in many other parish histories and would be tedious.

Some other village inhabitants

What does emerge, particularly after the seventeenth century, is the failure of names to persist. Families were clearly more mobile than is sometimes thought, and this will have been partly because of the paucity of yeoman farms. Taken together with a high failure rate of family succession it becomes rare for a family to survive even a hundred years in the parish. In such circumstances, repeated in successive centuries, the 'continuity' of the countryside becomes a concept rather subtler than generally understood, if indeed it existed at all. Local traditions, if such there were, will have had to be passed by example or word of mouth to unrelated people. It is a tenuous concept in Easthorpe, and rural 'tradition' in the accepted sense may always have been hard to find.

One much more modern allusion must be made. The accession of George Bush to the Presidency of the United States in January 1989 caused local excitement: his ancestry has been stated as having been traced to a Reynold Bush from the parish of Messing who sailed to Massachusetts on the 'Lion' in 1631 and who, it is presumed, was a son of John Bush of the same parish. The name 'Bush' is in fact to be found in several local parishes in the previous century, including Copford, Birch and Feering. Several such references have religious connections and illustrate the standing of the family in the parish; in 1524, for example, John Bushe was warden of the Lady Guild of Birch, holding its 'stok', while in 1553 Thomas Bushe is given as churchwarden of Messing. John is the most frequent name in the family and probably will most usually have been given to the eldest son as was customary.

It is therefore of obvious interest that Easthorpe should have a series of early seventeenth century references to the name of Bush, whilst possessing none in the sixteenth. The first mention is of a John Bush, son of John Bush, as baptised at Easthorpe Church in 1606. He appears to have been followed by no fewer than six brothers, the last in 1621. A John Bush, probably but not necessarily the elder, is buried in 1626. Thereafter no more references to male members of the family occur at all though Anne Bushe has a bastard daughter baptised in 1631 ('Wm Hilles reputed father') and Alice marries into the Puritan family of Damyon in 1633 and a Phyllis marries in 1636.

The most likely explanation of the abrupt arrival and departure of John Bush and his family is that he took the lease of a farm and that that lease fell in or was given up soon after his death. The question then arises of which that farm might have been, and it happens that there are only three in the parish which do not have certain or likely known inhabitants at the relevant dates: they are Fouchers, adjacent to Feering, Canfields and Winterfloods. These latter two, it will be recalled from earlier chapters not only lie along the lane between Easthorpe and Messing but are actually islands of Easthorpe intermingled with the latter parish, but while circumstantial evidence of the Messing connections favours one or other of these as the home of John Bush others of that name are known from Feering. No certain connection can, of course, be traced to Reynold Bush but it is likely that he knew both the farm and the family, and it is notable that his own story suits well with the strongly puritan Easthorpe tradition.

Chapter Nine

THE SURROUNDINGS OF THE PARISH

The limits of any parish history are not only self-imposed but are entirely artificial. In the case of Easthorpe, where the detached parts of the parish make its boundaries so unusual, restriction within them gives an exceptionally partial picture. Like any other parish, Easthorpe was subject to many major influences, some of them located close to its borders, without reference to which its history cannot properly be understood. This chapter accordingly seeks to put it just a little more into context through a few observations about the surrounding area. These observations are highly selective and certainly by no means exhaustive.

It has already been remarked that the closeness of the village to the main London road must always have been of great significance in daily parish life. The inhabitants were responsible for the maintenance of only a hundred yards of it and tackled their task with little enthusiasm, but this should have seemed a small price to pay for being so close to news of the world outside. As for actually hearing that news, the best place was unquestionably the Trowel and Hammer (more recently the Spaniard, and now demolished), which originally stood some twenty yards in front of the present building on what is now the westerly carriageway of the A12. A footpath from Little Birch Holt takes the Easthorpe pedestrian to Potts Green, and from there the Trowel and Hammer is only a short step. Local inhabitants still recall how well this path was used during the thirty years between the closing of the Bell and the opening of the No Name.

The heyday of the Trowel and Hammer was the heyday of droving, as it was on the main route for animals being driven to the London markets, notably geese from Norfolk. It became a well-known stop-over point for the drovers, having four acres behind it on which the geese were penned. At one time it possessed more land further afield. The earliest mentions of its use by drovers are from around 1700, but it was certainly an alehouse in 1623 and may well have even earlier origins.

To the east of the village, as the land becomes lower and heavier, the road was once very much wider than it is today. As elsewhere, this was because wheeled traffic sought to avoid impassable or damaging ruts; field boundaries, at whatever period they were fixed, respected this established necessity. The highway itself seems nevertheless to have been understood to have been at about its present width, because land outside it was waste of the manor. The cottages which line it today, like those which border the lane from Dawsons Green to Copford, were built by permission of the manor of Copford between 1740 and 1840. Their long, thin gardens still clearly show their origins.

One such house stands a little further back and has an early history. This is Kildegaard, once Postell Pightle. The house itself was rebuilt some thirty years ago, but existing photographs of it before this time show it to be of the long and low type of cottage once typical of the parish and the district. Its appearance was very similar to that of Joyes, which stood not far away. It is particularly interesting to note that the

The surroundings of the parish

Postell Pightle

name Postell Pightle was transferred to the house from a meadow adjoining, and that its original (or sixteenth century) name was Strat Enclos — Street Enclosed — later corrupted, amusingly enough, to Stratford and Uncles. Postell Pightle figures in the will of John Hunwick of Little Birch Holt in 1594, and it was subsequently sold by Parnell Ellis, widow, and Peter Ellis her son (then living at the Stanway Swan) to John Commyns (occupier) and Robert Ham. John Hunwick may perhaps have been related to the Anwykes, mentioned under Hazells, but the family is prominent in Colchester at this date. John Commyn's share eventually descended to John Vinson, blacksmith of Beckton in Suffolk, who sold it to Thomas Ham in 1631. Until recent years Postell Pightle thereafter had no independent existence.

Between Postell Pightle and Dawsons Green, on the same side of the road as the house but a hundred yards or so away from it, a number of hollows are reported or reputed. Dowsing has indicated that some of these equate to shapes of buildings. There have, too, been finds of pottery, unglazed but in quantity. Much lead and also much clinker has been discovered, together with a number of other objects. It seems likely from the nature of these finds that some mediaeval industrial site was here, and excavation would no doubt reveal exactly what. A little further on, close to Dawsons Green, there was an irregular field, known as Old Potters Field, which may perhaps have been connected in some way with this other site.

Dawsons Green itself is named after a family who farmed the adjoining fields at the time of the Commonwealth. The name Dawsons Lane used to be applied to the track, still a footpath, which runs from Dawsons Green towards Hellens: this was anciently the road to Layer Marney. The green was at one time of considerable size, and the present simple-looking road junction was then a much more complex affair, as old maps show. In particular, the lane to Copford once went round the plot upon which the council houses now stand facing the crossing: this site was a small field known as Bedlames or earlier Beldames. In 1752 Daniel Burdox was allowed to dig up part of Dawsons Green. Thereafter a number of cottages were built on it or at its edges, and although all are now demolished the sites of two are still clearly identifiable. One other stood at the side of Dawsons Lane, against Old Potters Field.

The surroundings of the parish

Down the lane from Dawsons Green towards Hoggets stands Whitehouse Farm. This name is certainly as early as the seventeenth century and no previous name is known. Its early connection with Great Birch Hall has already been mentioned, but no other details of its mediaeval history can be traced. Its later history is mainly one of descent through the female line. From split inheritance by the three daughters of Mark Mott, rector of Rayne, it was through part purchases gradually pieced together again by Thomas Kemp, originally of Foxearth and later of Birch Hall. By 1665 he had it all and John Cockerell was the occupier. At the time of his death in 1692 all his children were already dead except his daughter Sarah. She lived to be old, dying a widow in 1755, and the property passed to her only daughter, another Sarah, married to Richard Whitfield. Sarah and her husband did not hold the property long, dying in 1765 and 1766 respectively. Their only son, Richard, inherited Whitehouse but died at the early age of 27 ten years later, and the property passed to a sister married to Richard Pindar, goldsmith, of Aldersgate Street in London. In 1783 Pindar was declared bankrupt and Whitehouse was sold to James Hodgkin, tobacco broker, of Distaff Lane, again of course in London. Hodgkin's family held it until selling it to James Round in 1811, when the solicitors handling the sale found that the deeds were largely illegible. They had been kept in a tin box in a cellar and having become wet had foolishly been dried in the sun by a maidservant. None of these owners resided but the occupiers are known: from 1720 they are William Whitlock, William Burdox, William Shippey, Isaac Bedford, William Carter, William Brewer, John Brewer, and (1831 on) Langley Smyth.

Whitehouse

Along the lane from Dawsons Green to Heckfordbridge stands Boarded Barns. It received this name in the nineteenth century, when no doubt some sensitive resident decided that the earlier name of Bawd's Barn was unacceptable. Confusingly it appears that the name "The Boarded Barn" had earlier been applied to Beldhams field at Dawsons Green, usually Bawd's Barn property. On which of the two sites the barn itself stood is not certain, but Beldhams is much the more likely. In 1770 "Bawd's Barn" was

The surroundings of the parish

occupied by Daniel Gilder (mentioned under Canfields) and owned by Charles Gray (his Canfields landlord), and at this time occurs the phrase "the said barn being many years demolished". In 1732 the barn is described as "recently demolished", while in 1700 it is apparent that the barn was still standing and mention is made of the earlier name of Rayners, presumably attributable again to Beldhams field.

The name "Beldhams" may again be a politer version of Bawds, which in fact has an early origin. Joan Baud is the earliest certain owner of the land in this area. She was the wife of William Baud as early as 1350, marrying him as widow and heiress of Walter de Pattishall, who had died in 1330. A Henry Baud is shown for Easthorpe or Birch in the Lay Subsidy of 1327.

Leaving Boarded Barns for Heckfordbridge the lane skirts a house known as Basketts, built in a field of the same name. Not far away lies the site of a forgotten little farm called Elders, at the sharp bend of the lane between Basketts and Copford. In the other direction another small farm lay close to the narrow lane leading to Copford Church. Much more important than any of these is Bockingham Hall, a principal house of the district.

The detailed history of Bockingham Hall is outside the scope of this book, but some facts are relevant. Its connection with the distant Flispes has already been mentioned and has no obvious explanation except as an ancient holding. Bockingham is often stated, albeit on little positive evidence, to have been of importance in Saxon times, and it is certainly interesting to note that this Saxon 'ham' name should be separated from its Flispes possession by a Danish 'thorp' name — but what this tells of settlement or social history is difficult to interpret. In later times it was held by the de Bottinghams until the marriage of their heiress to Edward de Tey; Sir Robert de Tey, who died in 1426, held it of the Abbot of St. John's, Colchester. Its history following its sale by Thomas Tey in 1576 was chequered and fraught with dispute. It passed through many hands, including those of the Audeleys (mentioned under Badcocks), and then appears to have had a papist connection. Francis Butler refused to take the Papists' Disabling Oath in 1669, and Nathaniel Piggott of Middle Temple, papist, had a schedule of his lands taken in 1717; these included Flispes. Butler had left Bockingham Hall to his nephew, Ambrose Mandeville, but Nathaniel Piggott became possessed of it through Butler's subjecting it "to the payment of debts and legacies which are unpaid or unsatisfied". Even so, after Piggott's death it reverted to the Mandevilles, all resident in Ireland. The lawyer Charles Gray, who significantly enough was also believed to have Jacobite sympathies, was for many years involved in the complex affairs of Bockingham Hall, and in 1727 secured it for himself, so effectively ending the lawsuits. Since his time it has remained with the Round family.

In addition to Flispes, ownership of Bockingham Hall always brought with it "a cottage at Heckfordbridge", but it was not the only manor to have had an interest in this ancient crossing. The bridge itself is believed to be the origin of the name Birch or 'bric', and it lies only a little below the Roman crossing of the river at Gol Grove. Easthorpe manor had a longstanding interest in what the records consistently call a woodstack, subject to the manorial rent of 6d. For many years this woodstack was the responsibility of the Oddys, the blacksmiths, which presumably reflects the relative scarcity at Easthorpe of wood for the forge when compared with the plenty of the Roman river.

The surroundings of the parish

From Heckfordbridge a lane leads to the ruins of Little Birch Church. It stood at one end of this poor and fragmented parish, and its only chance of prosperity lay in its proximity to the hall. Unfortunately, although the hall was a building of some

Little Birch Church

importance it was usually tenanted, and few of its inhabitants took much apparent interest in the church. By 1600 it was becoming ruinous, but during the 1630s was re-roofed and generally improved by John Eldred of Birch Hall together with Lady Swinnerton of Stanway Hall. Eldred apparently intended it to serve as a funeral chapel, and a number of Eldred monuments were erected. During the Commonwealth, however, it again became ruinous, so that by the time James Round purchased Birch Hall in 1724 it was apparently considered too far gone to be worth restoring. Instead it was left as a picturesque ruin, and its tower appears in many prints of the hall even when the view is taken from a standpoint from which the tower could not possibly have been seen. Little Birch never had a rectory, and in 1610 the glebe was reported to be worth only £5 8s. per annum and the tithes only £15. Great and Little Birch were eventually united by Act of Parliament, and the church became private property in 1813.

There have been at least three halls on the site. Early in the seventeenth century the hall was described as "a very ancient edifice built chiefly by the Tendring and Golding families, and adorned by nine escutcheons of their arms". James Round demolished this hall in 1724 and built what from contemporary prints appears as a very handsome structure, and not one of too large a size. That perhaps proved its undoing, as it was itself demolished in 1843 in favour of a much more grandiose and sprawling building, which Pevsner described as an Italianate villa in Gothic style. Had it not been built the Rounds might still have been living at Birch Hall today, but instead this last, rather inconvenient building was pulled down in 1954. The senior representative of the line, Lt. Col. J. G. Round, now lives at Hellens near Hardys Green.

The name of Hellens is a trap for the unwary local historian. The property was owned by the family of Hellen, and before that was rented by them at least as early as 1778, in which year James Hellen paid William Sturgeon the considerable sum of £102, and it might therefore be supposed that it took its name from them. This, however, is not so. Its earlier name was Helions, and it was usually called Great Helions, in order to distinguish it from Little Helions, a property near Great Birch church: the ownership of

The surroundings of the parish

the two was split in the seventeenth century. The Hellen family must have enjoyed the joke. Against Hellens a field on the Shemmings side of the house was a site for potash burning, and a kiln stood there for many years.

Not far from Hellens is Beckingham Hall, but this name was given the house at its rebuilding. Its previous name was Howfield or Gravel Pit Say. A tenement there was described as "lately built" in 1685, and it adjoined the "great barne now or late of Gilbert Milbank". This was perhaps the attractive barn which stood close to the existing house until its demolition only a few years ago.

The oldest house adjoining Hardy's Green itself, and an older house than Beckingham Hall, is Webbs and Wells. The house is clearly identifiable by its white weatherboarding, but its name has been forgotten and the fabric has been drastically renewed. Its history is clear from the late seventeenth century when it was connected with the family of Damyon, already mentioned under Spicers. The Damyons were strict Puritans, and it is likely that the meeting house licence granted in 1672 to "Zachary Damyon's house in Birch Magna" is a reference to Webbs and Wells; the leading Presbyterian influence at this time was the Haynes family, of Copford Hall and Old Holt. Webbs and Wells was not then a large farm and cannot have been viable as an independent holding. Thomas Thedam is recorded as the occupier around the year 1700, and a certain John Dow in 1708, Dow's sister Elizabeth having a half share in it after her death. When John Damyon died in 1776 the house went to his widow Elizabeth, whose maiden name was Dow. The name of her next husband was Wadley, a name still common locally, and the property eventually passed to their two daughters. In 1834 Webbs and Wells was sold by Abraham Hardy of Tollesbury to Robert Levett of Beckingham Hall, and became a cottage for labourers on the farm.

Opposite the drive to Hellens a track may still be seen leading to a patch of trees where until recent years stood the ancient farmstead of Poynants. The name is mediaeval, presumably linking to a John Poynant of Great Birch mentioned in a deed of 1417 and to a Richard Poynant of 1327, but its history is obscure in detail because it ceased to be an independent holding at an early date, becoming part of Shemmings. This was certainly so after the time of John Daniel of Messing, the same mentioned under Hazells and elsewhere, who owned Poynants with ten acres from his inheritance in 1508 till his death in 1556. In 1741, however, Poynants seems to have been independent again and its tenant was Richard Hellen; this is the earliest mention of that family in the immediate vicinity. In 1764 it became one of the many properties to fall into the hands of William Sturgeon, then rapidly building up an estate, but after the early death in 1778 of his son, resident at Tolleshunt Darcy, the estate was dispersed through the female line. Poynants never rose again above a farm cottage. The history of the later Sturgeons is well seen on the wall tablets of Copford Church; earlier they lived for many years at Hill Farm, Copford, known at that time as Nevards.

Further up the lane, just before the "Great Pond" opposite Shemmings, stood Thedams Farm, as has already been mentioned under the histories of Hoggets and other properties. Its earliest known name, remembered for centuries in the names of certain fields, was the Hay and Starlings, this occurring at least as early as 1430. It is an intriguing title because 'Haie' is the Norman French name for 'enclosure' while 'Starlings' can have several meanings but could refer to spiked pales. Some of the field names of this farm are evocative: "the mowing field", "the two misling fields", "Dorrance pit". The family named Thedam or Thedham had a long history in the area

The surroundings of the parish

from Thomas Thedam of Layer Marney (c. 1500) to George Thedam of Flispes in the 1880's and beyond that to the present day. The branch at Thedams Farm was certainly there from 1600 and possibly earlier: from them we have an unusually complete series of wills. The last Thomas Thedam of Thedams was obliged to borrow £450 against the value of the farm from William Sturgeon, and in consideration of this left it to the same man, described as "his good friend" and "farmer and grazier". The house is shown on a map of 1773 drawn up for the second William Sturgeon, but appears to have been demolished soon afterwards and no trace of it is visible today.

Shemmings itself used to be known as Bullens and Shemmyns (or Bollyngs and Chimmyns, or other variants). The latter is the correct name for the house, and references to Hamo and to Richard Chymyn occur in the assize rolls of 1262 and the Feet of Fines in 1338. Bollings was a holding behind Shemmings, between it and Palmers; a John Bollyn is mentioned in 1430, but whether there was ever a dwelling is uncertain. One interestingly named field which became part of Shemmings in about 1670 was The Morrey or more anciently Le Morrice, a Norman French name bearing comparison with the "Haie" nearby.

The land farmed with Shemmings varied greatly. The original holding appears to have been mostly to the east of the house, including, for example, Crossfield, which it owned until about 1660; but by the time of John Bridges, owner in 1784, its hundred acres lay almost entirely to the west. Frequent changes of ownership and the rarity of owner occupiers are probably the reasons. By the middle of the last century this fine old house had at length ceased to operate as an independent farm and had declined into three labourers' lets.

Palmers Farm lies not far from the Maldon Road and is older than the generally eighteenth century appearance it presents today. Reaney in his "Place Names of Essex" derives the name from a Roger Palmer mentioned in 1346, and it is certain that a Richard Palmer was there at the end of the fifteenth century. Thomas Peverill came next, possibly a relative of the Peverills mentioned under the "No Name". During the mid part of the seventeenth century it was owned by Hezekiah Haynes of Old Holt, becoming the subject of a marriage settlement in 1681. After passing thereafter through several hands rather quickly it attained its principal claim to fame through its ownership by the actor David Garrick: the lands in his possession extended almost to Sandford Hall Green. David Garrick the elder is first recorded as having possession in 1771, and by marriage settlement it passed to David Garrick the younger in 1778. The Garricks also owned Clarke's Farm at Ardleigh.

From Palmers Farm the quickest way back to Easthorpe is along the straight concrete road, once a runway of Birch Airfield, which follows approximately the course of the old Blind Lane. The name is still sometimes used locally to describe the new road. When the runway was constructed the cottages which stood half way along Blind Lane were demolished, and so too was a small and late farm, near Sandfordhall Green. The derivation of the name "Sandfordhall" itself is not clear, because so many Sandfords or Samfords owned land in the area at various times. It is certainly older than the Benjamin Sanford who owned the land in the 1780s. Reaney even thinks it likely that the derivation is from a John Sandford mentioned in the Calendar of Close Rolls in 1413.

The surroundings of the parish

One of the puzzles of Sandfordhall is whether there was an early dwelling on the site. The present house is quite modern, but in 1778 we find that there is a £2 15s rent for "Sanford House". In 1789, however, it is clear that the property consisted of "a barn and fifty acres" described as "once waste of the manor but many years since enclosed". The barn has many subsequent references and certainly existed, but no positive reference to a house occurs till comparatively recent times. The name Sandfordhall goes back at least to the seventeenth century, but the reference to manorial waste is difficult to explain if an earlier dwelling is postulated. The earliest discoverable reference does not refer to a hall at all; in 1622 the inhabitants of Great Birch and Messing were presented at Quarter Sessions on the grounds that "the highways are most dangerous between Messing Hall and Sandford Grene". This suggests that the present footpath between Canfields and Sandfordhall Green was a through route; it does not say "between Messing Hall and Easthorpe", as might have been expected. A possible explanation of the "hall" is that it was a variant of the common rural "hundred acre" joke about tiny fields.

Even today no house stands between Messing Hall and Canfields, the long and lonely stretch of road suggesting that the land remained unsettled in early times. Indeed, it is notable throughout the annals of the parish that with the exceptions of Hazells Farm and of William Miles' ownerships there has been hardly any historical connection between Messing and Easthorpe. Inter-marriages were rare and branches of one family are not often to be found in both villages, a situation in strong contrast with Easthorpe's relationship to Birch or to Copford. There continues even now to be little Easthorpe connection with Messing. Perhaps it is the continuing difficulty of travelling that long lane which caused trouble in 1622, but it is tempting to think that it is just the pervasive continuity of history.

INDEX

Abbotts Field, 42
Alane, Henry, 38
Alderman, John, 42
Amerie
    Abigail, 65
    Grace, 65
    John, 64, 65
    Lawrence, 64
    Richard, 64
    William, 64
Anwyke family, 92
Anwyke,
    Alice, 70
    Richard, 70
    Thomas, 70
Applebee,
    John, rector, 23, 35
    Maria, 23, 35
Ardleigh,
    John, of Great Birch, 76
    John, of Flispes, 52, 76, 88
    John (of Aldham), 76
    Nicholas, 76
    William, 76
Ashe, Anthony, 77
Atkins, Richard, 19, 20
Audeley family, 94
Audeley,
    Katherine, 18, 37, 38, 76, 77
    Katherine, daughter-in-law, 38
    Robert, 38
    Sir Thomas, Lord Chancellor of England, 18, 38
    Thomas, nephew, 18, 38
Ayloff, William, 74

Bacon,
    John (various holders of the name), 19, 75
    Elizabeth, mother, 74, 75
    Elizabeth, daughter, 75
    Thomas, father, 74, 75
    Thomas, son, 75
Badcock, John, 37
Badcocks, 12, 16, 18, 37-41, 44, 45, 47, 48, 51, 55, 57, 74, 75, 76, 77, 80, 81, 82, 83, 89, 94, illustrated 37
Badcocks, Great, see Badcocks
Badcocks, Little, 7, 38, 41-5, 55, 69, 77, 78, 80, 85, 88, illustrated 41
Baker,
    Elizabeth, 23, 35
    John, 23, 35
Bards (Beards), 55
Barnard, Mary, 54
Baron, Simon, 29
Barrington, John, 43
Basketts, 94
Baud,
    Joan, 88, 94
    Henry, 43
    William, 88, 94
Bauds Barn, see Boarded Barns
Baynard family, 27, 71
Baynard, Richard, 17, 27, 31
Baysey,
    John, 42
    Francis, 46
Beal, John, rector, 33, 43
Beards, see Bards
Beaumont family, 86
Beaumont,
    Gameliel, rector, 28, 32
    Stephen, father, rector, 19, 32, 74, 88
    Stephen, son, 32
    Susannah, 32
Beaumont Field, 12
Beckingham Hall (Howfield, Gravel Pit Say), 15, 55, 96, 97
Bedlames (Beldhams), 92, 93
Bell, public house, 10, 61, 65, 91, illustrated, 61
Bell Cottage, see Bell, public house
Biggs, Thomas, 56
Binder, John, 74
Birch, Sarah, 72
Birch, 14, 46, 53, 54, 55, 57, 61, 67, 74, 76, 77, 90, 93, 95, 96
    Castle, 14, 15, 17, 73
    Hall, 15, 18, 22, 88, 93, 95
Birch, Great, 14, 20, 42, 46, 48, 54, 66, 67, 68, 73, 75, 86, 88, 92, 98
    Church, 26, 29, 32
    Hall, 15
    Manor, 15
Birch, Little, 14, 19, 43, 45, 65, 70, 76
    Church, 26, 33, 68, 95, illustrated 94
    Hall, 15, 18, 19, 44, 95
    Holt, 22, 28, 64, 77, 91
Birches, William a, 14

99

Index cont.

Blagrave, Edward, 21
Blind Lane, 97
Blosse,
    John, 56
    Philip, 56
Blowers,
    John, 59, 72
    Thomas, 59, 72
Blund, William, 16
Blandford, Elizabeth, 23
Boarded Barns, 88, 93
Bockingham Hall, 16, 72, 76, 77, 94
Bohun, Sir John de, 82
Bollings, 97
Bollyn, John, 97
Bonner, Bishop, 30
Bonner, Martha, 54
Bottingham, de, family, 94
Bottingham, Roger de, 76
Bottingham, Walter de, 88
Bourchier, John, 71
Bourchiers Hall, Messing, 16, 70, 71
Bover, Roger le, 17
Bowles,
    George, rector, 36, 78, illustrated 35
    George Herbert, 36
Boys,
    William, father, 34
    William, son, rector, 34-5
Brasier,
    Ann, 34, 35
    John, rector, 34, 39, 44
Brasier family, 66, 78, 83
Bredlesse Street, 64
Brewer,
    John, 93
    William, 93
Bridges, John, 97
Bright, Samuel, 75
Briset, Jordan, 81
Broadfield, 11
Browne, John, 76
Bullens and Shemmyns, see Shemmings
Bullock(e), Sir Edward, 47, 82
Bundocke, John, 86
Burdox,
    Daniel, 92
    William, 93
Bush,
    John, various holders of the name, 90
    George, President of the U.S.A., 90
    Reynold, 90

Bushe,
    Alice, 90
    Anne, 90
    John, 90
    Phyllis, 90
    Thomas, 90
Butler, Francis, 72, 77, 94
Buxton,
    Isaac, 74, 80, 81, 82
    John, 80
    Thomas, grandfather, 80
    Thomas, grandson, 80

Cable,
    Alice, 68
    Henry, 68
Calendar of Close Rolls (1413), 97
Calveswick (Calverwicke) ad Guildhall, 68
Campion, Isaac, 69
Canfields (Cawenfield, Cawens), 10, 16, 40, 46, 51, 54, 55-8, 73, 74, 89, 90, 94, illustrated 56
Carbins Lane, 55
Carder, Richard, 74
Carter,
    Samuel, 81
    William, 93
Cawenfield, see Canfields
Chambre, Thomas de la, 48
Chandler family, 33
Chandler,
    John, father, 52, 53-4
    John, son, 54
    Margaret, 54
    Martha, 54
Chatterton family, 44, 68, 79
Chatterton,
    Daniel, 79
    Francis, 43, 79
    John, 79
    Joanna, 79
    Robert, 79
Chibborne, Christopher, 70, 71, 74
Chinnery, William, 62, 63
Christmas,
    Anne, 80
    Lucy, 89
    Samuel, 66 89
Chymyn, Richard, 97
Clarke family, 50
Clarke,
    James, 47, 49, 50
    John, 47, 49

Index cont.

Thomas, 47
William, 20, 47, 50, 87
Cobb, Edward, 88
Cockerell,
    John, 93
    Sarah, mother, 93
    Sarah, daughter, 93
Codwill, Joan de, 88
Colchester Oath Book, 60, 67, 70
Committee of Plundered Ministers, 32
Commyns, John, 93
Conyers, John, 71
Cook,
    Mary, 23
    Thomas, 22
Cooke,
    Edward, 69
    Joseph, 44
    Robert, 69
    Susannah, 69
    William, 69
"Cooks Croft", see Great Guildhouse
Cope, Rev. Anthony, 50
Copford Green, 10, 51
Cordell, John, Rector of Copford, 42, 44
Cornwell, Susannah, 89
Cow Meadow, 23
Cox,
    John, 23
    Sarah, 89
    William, 86
Cranfield family, 47
Cranfield,
    John, 32, 87
    Mary, 86
    Richard, father, 86
    Richard, son, 87
Craxes, 21, 34
Creffield family, 40, 44
Creffield,
    Ann, 44
    Elizabeth, 44
Crispe, Robert, 18, 19
Crooke, Isaac, 47
Cross a Hand(tree), 47
Crosse House, see Well Cottage
Crossfield, 56, 97
Crouches Land, see Mulberry Green
Crumpton,
    Ann, 75
    Daniel, 82
    David, 75
Crutched Friars, 66

Currye, Richard, 59

Damyes, see Damyons
Damyon (Deamon) family, 33, 42, 59, 84, 96
Damyon,
    Elizabeth, 47
    Henry (elder), 84
    Henry (younger), 42
    John ("Demon, Damond"), 84
    Jonas, father, 84
    Jonas, son, 84
    Joseph, 84
    William, 84
    Zachary, 96
Damyons (residence), 42
Damyons Field, 11
Daniel,
    Alice, 71
    Edward, 71
    John, father, 71, 96
    John, son, 46, 55, 71
Davey,
    Christine, 88
    William, 88
Dawes, John, 53
Dawsons Green, 8, 10, 51, 91, 92, 93
Dawsons Lane, 92
Deamon family, see Damyon family
Death (Deeth) family, 42
Deeth, William, 42, 43
Dell, Mary, 53
Doddens (Doddings) Lane, 13
Dolfin, Walter, 7
Domesday Book, see Doomsday Book
Domsey Brook, 7, 10, 12, 15, 85; origin of name, 7
Domsey House, 7
Doomsday Book, 15, 16, 47
Doves, 70
Dow,
    Elizabeth, 96
    John, 96
Dowsett, Hezekiah, 59
Duffield family, 45
Duffield,
    Joseph, 44
    Thomas, 44
Durrant, William, 56
Dyn, Robert, rector, 29

Easthorpe, John of, 88
Easthorpe, William de, 88

101

Index cont.

Easthorpe, local pronunciation of name, 10; origin of name, 9; parish defined, 5
Easthorpe Church, 26-8, 45, 90, illustrated 26
    Croft, 52, 53
    Green Farm (Fouchers), 13, 20, 40, 46-48, 49, 57, 60, 77, 80, 82, 90, illustrated 46
    Hall (Hall Farm), 18, 19-25, 34, 35, 89, illustrated 14
    Manor, 14-19, 23
    Rectory, 7, 28-36
    Street, 13, 28, illustrated 9
Eatney (Eateney, Ettene) family, 76
Eatney,
    Ann, 76
    Elizabeth, 76
    John, 76
    Joshua, 86
    Richard, 76
    Steven, 77, 86
    William, 76
Edric, holds Easthorpe Manor, 15
Edwards,
    James, of Birch, 62
    James, rector, 66
    Matthew, 62, 85
Elders, 94
Eldred,
    Ann, 22, 23
    John, 95
Ellis,
    Parnell, 92
    Peter, 92
Eley,
    Anne, 47
    Daniel, 54
    Elizabeth, 57
    George, 54, 55
    Isaac, 54, 58
    John, 54, 57, 58
    Mary, 54
    Rhoda, 58
    Susannah, 57
    Susannah (1760-97), 89
    Thomas, 51, 88
    Thomas, of Feering, 57
    Thomas, of Hunts, 58, 63
    Thomas, tenant of Badcocks, 82
    William, various holders of the name, 40, 51, 54, 57, 89
Emorie family, see Amorie family

Esthalle, William de, 88
Ettene family, see Eatney family
Eustace, Earl of Boulogne, 16
Everett,
    Elizabeth, 89
    Esther, 89
    James, 89
    John (first), 89
    John (second), 89
    Joseph (first), 89
    Joseph (second), 89

Fann Wood, 28
Farrell, Edward, 65
Feet of Fines; of 1218, 76; of 1294, 81; 0f 1296, 70; of 1338, 96, of 1365, 37
Fellocks, see Filcocks
Fenne, atte,
    Simon, 41
    William, 41
Fennes, see Little Badcocks
Fering,
    Hughe de, 49
    Saker (Sayer) de, 49
Filcocks (Fellocks), 75, 81, 82-3; origin of name, 83, illustrated 82
Finney (Finnay), Robert, rector, 29
Firmin, Thomas, 35
Fisher,
    James, 66
    Uriah, 81
Fitzthomas,
    Captain, 40
    Rev W.E., 40, 82
Flanders and Georges, 62, 85
Fletcher, village name, 68
Flisp,
    Richard, burgess of Colchester, 76
    Richard, died 1419, 76
    Stephen, 76
Flispes, 16, 22, 36, 48, 52, 58, 59, 72, 73, 75-78, 82, 86, 88, 94, illustrated 75
Ford,
    Elizabeth, 74
    William, 74
Forster,
    Alice, 19
    George, 18
    Joan, 18
    Mary, 18
    Richard, 18

Index cont.

Robert, 88
Foster, Thomas, rector, 30, 31, 32, 42
Foucher,
    Robert, 46
    Roger, 46
    Thomas, 46
    William, 46
Fouchers, see Easthorpe Green Farm
Fowcher,
    William (elder), 46
    William (younger), 46
Foxe's Book of Martyrs, 30
Francis,
    Barbara, 83
    John (father), 83
    John (son), 81, 83
    Rachael, 83
Freeman, Abraham, 77
French, William, 72
Fuller, Priscilla, 86
Furley, John, 71, 80

Gant family, 72
Gants, see Hazells
Gare,
    Adam de la, 76
    Cil'es de la, 76
    William de la, 76
Garlands, see Gernons, also Winnings
Garmond,
    John, 62
    Mary, 62, 85
Garrard (Garrod),
    Ann, 89
    Martha, 54, 89
    Thomas, 54, 89
Garrick,
    David (father), 97
    David (son), 97
George,
    John, 85
    Robert, 38, 85
Georges Croft (Flanders and Georges), 38, 62, 85
Gernon family, 14, 17, 27, 29, 73, 76, 78
Gernons (Garlands) 14, 15, 44
Giblin, Joseph, 81
Gilder,
    Daniel (father), 57, 89, 94
    Daniel (son), 57, 89
    Daniel (grandson), 89
    Elizabeth, 57
    Mary (mother), 89
    Mary (daughter), 89
    Thomas, 57
Glascock family, 79
Godfrey, Jacob, 53
Golding family, 19, 25
Golding,
    Arthur, 19, 43
    Henry, 19
    John (father), 78
    John (son), 78
Goodall family, 75
Goodall,
    John, 65, 87
    William, 87
Goodwin family, 52, 53, 62
Goodwin,
    John, various holders of the name, 52, 67, 88
    Nicholas, 67, 88
Goodwins, see No Name Public House
Gosbecks, 8
Gravel Pit Say, see Beckingham Hall
Gray, Charles, 48, 56, 57, 77, 93, 94
Gray, Wiliam, 29
Graye, Miles, 29
Great Badcocks, see Badcocks
Great Guildhouse (Cooks Croft), 27-28, 59, 62, 66-69, 85, 88
Green family, 23, 24, 34
Green,
    Anne, 50
    Elizabeth, 50
    Isaac, 44
    John, 22
    Mary, 22, 23, 50
    Mary, née Duffield, 44
    Robert, 22
    Thomas (father), 22, 23
    Thomas (son), 23, 50
    Thomas (first husband of Mary Barnard), 54
Grene family, 69
Grene,
    John, 68
    John, of Colchester, 70
    Letitia, 70
Gresham, Richard, 18
Grimston, David, 39
Grimston, third Viscount, Earl of Verulum, 51
Guildhouse, Great, see Great Guildhouse
Guildesborough family, 27, 66

Index cont.

Gusterson, Elizabeth, 40, 48
    Henry, 40, 41
    Margaret, 40
Guyblon, Thomas, 67

Hales (Hails), John, 72
Hall, Thomas, 40, 41
Hall Farm, see Easthorpe Hall
Hallbread, Daniel, 25, 79
Hallbread, John, rector, 35, 36
Halls, John, rector, 35, 74
Halls, Robert, 35
Hallward, John, rector, 35, 66
Ham family, 62
Ham,
    Margaret, 62
    Mary, 71
    Robert, 62, 68, 92
    Thomas (father), 62
    Thomas (son), 62, 92
    William, 71
Hardy, Abraham, 96
Hardys Green, 8, 10, 51, 95
Harrington,
    Andrew, 59
    Henry, 42
Harris, John, 81
Hasille,
    John, 76
    Robert, 76
Haynes family, 96
Haynes, Hezekiah, 23, 97
Hay and Starlings, see Thedams Farm
Hazells (Gants), 16, 46, 48, 49, 50, 57, 59, 70-2, 85, 88, 89, 92, 96,
Hearth Tax: of 1662, 65, 68, 77, 84; of 1672, 68, 74, 83
Heckfordbridge, cottage at, 94
Hellen,
    James, 95
    Richard, 96
Hellens (earlier Helions) Farm, 56, 12, 92 95, 96
Hewer,
    John, 41, 68, 88
    Robert, 42, 43
    Thomas (father), 42, 78
    Thomas (son), 42
Hewers, see Badcocks, Little
Heynes, Richard, 83-4
Hicks, John, 72
Hicks, tenement, 85

Highfields, 44
Hill,
    Elizabeth, 57
    William, 57
Hill Farm (Nevards), 23
Hillyer,
    Nathaniel (father), 23
    Nathaniel (son), 23, 25
    Susannah, 23, 25
Hodgkin, James, 93
Hoggets (Holdgates), 5, 10, 16, 24, 45, 48, 51-5, 57, 62, 88, 89, 93, 96, illustrated 52
Holdgate family, 53
Holdgates, see Hoggets
Holman, historian, 14
Holgrave, 59
Hollowbread, Thomas, 22
Horne, de, family, 60, 69
House without a Name, see No Name public house
Howfield, see Beckingham Hall
Hucks,
    Joseph, 51
    Sarah, 51
Hugh, under-tenant of Eustace, Earl of Boulogne, 15-16
Hunt, Hugh, 61, 82
Hunts, see No Name public house
Hurlebat, John, 88
Hurst,
    John, 71, 80, 81
    Joseph, 81
Hunwick, John, 92
Hutley family, 65
Hutley,
    John, 48
    Thomas, 44
    William, 55

Impey Estate, 55

Jackson, Mrs. Sarah, see Hucks, Sarah
Joggins, Mercy, 86
John, King, 16, 17, 29
Johnson,
    A., 75
    Dorothy, 33
    Thomas, rector, 21, 32
    Thomas, 39
Joslin family, 48
Joye,
    John, 78

Index cont.

Nicholas, 78
Peter, 17, 78
Simon, 80
Joyes, 44, 45, 69, 78-80, illustrated 79

"Karenci, Ibertus de", 16
Kidd, Robert, 78
Kidd, Thomas, 92
Kildegaard (Postell Pightle), 42, 91, illustrated 92
King, Thomas, 48
King, Thomas, of Flispes, 77
Kingsmill family, 19, 20, 21, 23
Kingsmill,
    Anna, 21, 22
    Anne, 21, 22, 34
    George, third son of Sir William, 21, 22, 34
    George, 20
Kingston,
    Bernard, 73, 74
    John, rector, 18, 29, 30, 31, 68, 73, 86

Ladham,
    Benjamin, 75
    Elizabeth, 75
Lamb,
    Charles, 87
    John, 87
Lanerymarsh, 84
Lawrence family, 20, 21
Lawrence,
    Anne, 20
    Aquilla, 20
    Elizabeth, 20
    Elizabeth Anna, 20
    John, 20
    Mary (wife of Thomas), 20
    Mary (daughter), 20, 47
    Nathaniel, 20
    Nathaniel (son), 20
    Sarah, 20
    Thomas, 19, 47
Lay Subsidy: of 1319-20, 87; of 1327, 49, 93; of 1380-1, 87; of 1524, 41, 53, 59, 62, 64, 67, 70, 84, 87
Leche, Robert, 84
Lester, John, rector, 29
Levett,
    Robert, 55, 96
    William, 56
Little Badcocks, see Badcocks, Little
Luckyn family, 50, 71
Lyster, John, rector, see Lester

Maltings Farm, 45; see also Badcocks, Little
Mandeville,
    Ambrose, 94
    Thomas, 83
March,
    Richard, 50
    Thomas, 50
Marney, Sir Henry, 46
Marshe, family, see March
Martham family, 41
May,
    John, father, 40, 48, 57
    John, son, 40, 57
    Mary, 40
    Richard, 40
    Susannah, 40, 57
    William, 40, 81, 82, 89
Mershton,
    Cecily de, 70
    Richard, 70
Middleton, Richard, 86
Miles,
    Edward, 62, 69
    James, 62
    William, 59, 60, 62, 69, 85
Millbank, Gilbert, 77, 96
Miller, John, 71
Mole, Mrs., 78
Moore,
    Wiliam (father), 57
    William (son), 57, 58
Morant, historian, 10, 14, 15, 17, 18, 21 23, 38, 66, 68
Moreton,
    Elizabeth, 65
    Robert, 65
Morrey, the (Le Morrice), 97
Moss, William, 66
Mott, Mark, rector of Rayne, 53, 92
Mulberry, Thomas, 66
Mulberry Green (Crouches Land), 10, 51, 62, 66
Murrell, Cunning, 78

Naillynghurst, Robert de, 71
Nelson, William, 68
Nevards, see Hill Farm
Nicholas, Rector, 29

105

Index cont.

No Name public house (Hunts, Peverills, Penrils, Goodwins), 24, 52, 58, 61-3, 66, 67, 68, illustrated 61, 83, 88 91, 60
Norris family, 59, 65
Nunscroft, 82

Oakleas, 44
Oddy family, 45, 94
Oddy,
    James, 65
    Solomon, 65, 66
    Thomas, 63, 65
Okeley, John, rector, 33
Old Potters Field, 92
Oliver, Oliver, rector, 29
Olivers, 22
Olivers, 70
Onslow family, 23
Onslow Cottages, 23, 66
Orchard Field, 23
Orpen, Lawrence, 48
Osborne family, 23, 35, 44, 45, tombs illustrated 24
Osborne,
    Catherine, 63
    Hannah, 40
    John (father), 24, 40, 63
    John (son), 24, 63, 84
    John (grandson), 24, 63
    Margaret, 89
    Thomas, 24
    William, various holders of the name, 19, 63
Owen,
    Christine (widow), 74
    John, 74

Palmer,
    Richard, 97
    Roger, 97
Palmer's Farm, 97
Parker,
    Alice, 68
    Anne, 68
    Jane, 68
    Michael, 68
    Richard, 62, 68
    Robert, 67, 68, 69, 88
    Thomas, 67
    Widow, 67, 88
Pattishall, Walter de, 93

Paul, Obadiah, rector, 21, 22, 33-4, 39, 42, 43, 44, 59, 68, 75
Paycocks, Coggeshall, 80
Peacocks, 12, 74, 75, 80-1, 82
Pecock, Thomas, 80
Penrils, see No Name public house
Perient, Thomas, 68
Perry, William, 43
Peverill family, 61, 62, 97
Peyton family, 17, 27, 37
Phillibrowne, Daniel, 43, 44, 79
Phillips family, 22, 33, 77
Phillips,
    Ann, 78
    Elizabeth, 77
    John, various holders of the name, 21, 77, 78
    Susannah, 77
Piggott, Nathaniel, 77, 94
Pilgrome,
    Joan ("Mother Pilgrome"), 38, 39
    John, 38
Pindar, Richard, 93
Planes,
    Roger de, 16
    William de, 16
Polley family, 44, 45
Polley,
    Elizabeth, 89
    James, 45, 66, 75
    May, 88
    Thomas, 85
Poor of Kelvedon, 71, 85
Porchfield, see Portfield
Porter,
    Anna, 74, 75, 81
    Elizabeth, 39
    John (father), 39, 81, 83
    John (son), 39, 74
    Thomas, various holders of the name, 39, 40, 75, 80
    William, 51
Porters Green, 10, 51
Portfield, 28
Postell Pightle, see Kildegaard
Potter family, 28, 59, 60
Potter,
    Charles, 89
    Elizabeth, 25
    Isaac (father), 48
    Mary, 40
    Richard, 76, 89
    Sarah, 89

Index cont.

    Stephen, 48
    Susannah, 89
    William, various holders of the name, 24, 56, 60
Potts Green, 91
Pound Yard, 15
Powell,
    Elizabeth, 48
    Henry, 48, 60
    James, 48
    John, 48, 60
    Joseph, 55
    Mary, 40
Poynant,
    John, 96
    Richard, 96
Poynants, 56, 96
Pudney, Thomas, 32, 42-3
Purkiss, William, 32

Rand,
    Elizabeth, 21, 77
    Mary, 20
    Richard (father), 21, 22, 24, 77
    Richard (son), 21, 33, 43
Rawlins,
    Catherine, 59
    Elizabeth (mother), 59
    Elizabeth (daughter), 59
    John, 59
Rawlins, holding, 49, 50
Raymond,
    Daniel, 63, 83
    Thomas, 83
Raymonds,
    cottage, 85
    meadow, 83
Rayner, Sarah, 65
Rayners, barn, 94
Reade,
    George, 52
    Thomas, 52
Roo (Ros), Hugh, 88
Root family, 71
Ros, Hugh, see Roo, Hugh
Round family, 95
Round,
    James, 44, 92, 93, 95
    J.H., 14, 17
Ruffle, John, 84

St. Helen, Guild of, 66
St. John of Jerusalem, Knights Hospitallers of, 81
St. Johns Garden, 61, 75, 81-2, 83
St. Mary, Guild of, 66
St. Quintin,
    Hugh de, 16
    Seive de, 16
Salmon, Widow, 50
Salmons, 50, 71 (see also Rawlins)
Sanchye, William, 18
Sandford,
    Benjamin, 97
    John, 97
Sandford Green, 10, 15, 51, 53, 97, 98
Saundford, John and Matilde de, 49
Scott,
    John, 49
    Mary, 49
    William, 49
Scottard, Walter, 49
Scotties (Scottards, Scotlives), 10, 47, 48-51 57, 58, 59, 70, 71, 72, 73, 81
    illustrated 49
Seabrook, village name, 66
Searle family, 65
Segg, Thomas, rector, 29
Selly, Elizabeth, 35
Sharrer, Susannah, 23
Shave,
    John, 21, 28, 43
    Priscilla (mother), 43
    Priscilla (daughter), 43
    Sarah, 43
    Thomas, 43, 44, 77
Shelton, John, 59, 88
Shemmings (Bullens and Shemmyns), 44, 48, 53, 77, 96, 97
Shepherd,
    Rev. George, 40
    Samuel, 40
Sherwood family, 25, 40, 41, 46, 51
Ship Money, 65, 68
Siggens, Walter, 66
Skynns, 71
Slarvery Marsh, 7
Smith,
    Ann, 71, 85
    Daniel (father), 25
    Daniel (son), 25
    James, 85
    John, 40
    Robert, 71, 85

Index cont.

Susannah, 25
Smyth, Langley, 93
Spaniard public house, see Trowel and Hammer
Sparrow, Samuel, 75, 82
Spendlove, John, 88
Spice (Spicer) family, 27, 66, 83
Spice,
    Alice, 83
    Clement (elder), 66, 83
    Clement (younger), 83
    Richard, 83
    Roger, 83
Spicers, 27, 83, 95
Spillman, Peter, 76
Spring,
    Joan, 68
    Robert, 18, 43, 68
Springett family, 72
Stane Street, 86
Stanton, Edward, 86
Stebbing,
    Ann, 45
    George, 45
    George Hutley, 45
Stebbing,
    Thomas, 11
    William, 11
Steele, Widow, 43, 44
Stegg, John, 88
Stilliman, John, 56
Stonnard (Stonard),
    Anthony, 55, 56
    John, 56
    John, 56, 74
    Thomas, 20
Strat Enclos (Stratford and Uncles), 92
Stretecroft (Street Croft), 84, 85
Sturgeon estate, 48, 55
Sturgeon, William, 95, 96
Sutton,
    John de, 70
    Phillipa de, 70
    Robert, 76
    Thomas, 70
    Thomas de, 70
Suttons Lane, 70

Tabor, Joseph, 86
Taylor,
    Joseph, 43, 44
    Samuel, 44
Taysgill, George and Hannah, 48

Templar, Knights, 81
Tendring family, 95
Tendring, Ralph de, 70, 78
Terrier of 1637, 5, 12, 28, 44, 59, 71
Tey family, 37, 38, 76
Tey,
    Edward de, 94
    Sir Robert de, 94
    Thomas, 38, 88, 94
    William, 84
Thedam family, 44, 48, 96, 97
Thedam,
    George, 97
    Lydia, 44
    Thomas, 96, 97
    William, 44, 53
Thedams Farm (Hay and Starlings), 44, 48, 55, 96, 97
Theedham, George, 48
Theobald family, see Tibball family
Theobald, Sarah, 77
Thompson, Peter, 56
Tibball (Tibbald) famiy, 50, 59
Tibball,
    Elizabeth, 50
    John, 50
    John (died 1720), 51
    Rachel, 50
    Richard, 50
    Thomas (father), 50, 78
    Thomas (son), 78
Tiler (Tyler),
    Alice, 70
    Christopher, 70
    John, various holders of the name, 70, 71
    Richard, 70, 88
"Tone and his Wife", 88
Townsend, 74, 75
Traveller's burial at Easthorpe, 89
Trowel and Hammer public house (Spaniard), 91
Triggs, field, 11
Turnage,
    John, 57
    Thomas, 57
Turner family, 39, 44, 47, 80
Turner,
    Hannah, 39
    Joan, 39
    Peter, 39, 47
    Thomas (father), 39
    Thomas (son), 39, 47

Index cont.

Turners, 55 (see also Bards or Beards)
Turrell, Elizabeth, 57
Twede family, 37, 88
Twede,
    Nicholas, 88
    Richard, 88
    William, 88
Tyall, John, 70
Tyrell, Sir Henry, 71

Verulam, Earl of, see Grimston, third Viscount
Vesye,
    Alice, 67, 68
    William, 67, 68, 80, 88
Vinson, John, 92

Wade,
    Elizabeth, 44
    Elizabeth, born 1748, 89
    James, 89
    John, 89
    Lydia, 44, 79
    Mary (mother), 89
    Mary (three daughters), 89
    Mira, 41
    Robert, 86
    Thomas, 41
    William, various holders of the name, 44, 55
Wakering, John, 85
Waldegrave, Robert, 18, 19
Walford, Ambrose, 72
Walle,
    Nicholas (father), 46, 47
    Nicholas (son), 46, 47
    Nicholas (grandson), 47
Wardner, Edmund, 86
Webb, John, 86
Wegg,
    George, 51
    Samuel, 51
Well Cottage (Crosse House), 7, 23, 28, 45, 50, 58, 59, 61, 63-6, 89, illustrated 64
Well Lane, 7, 59, 61, 64, 68, 83, 85
Wharton family, 38, 47
Wharton,
    Andrew, 39
    Joan, 38
    John, 38
    Margaret, 38
    Robert, 38
    Thomas, 39
Whitehouse (White House) Farm, 15, 92, illustrated 93
Whitfield,
    Richard (father), 93
    Richard (son), 93
Whiting, John, rector, 33
Whitlock, William, 93
Wingfield, John, 84
Winnings, 20, 31, 56, 68, 73-5, 85
Winterflod, Ralph de, 58
Winterfloods, 7, 10, 16, 24, 40, 56, 58-60, 69, 73-5, 85, 89, 90, illustrated 58
Woodward family, 52, 53
Woodward,
    Henry, 88
    John, 53
    Rebecca, 53
    Robert, 52
    Thomas, 53
    William, 52, 53
Wordsworth, Robert, 74
Wright,
    Joan, 73
    John, (father), 73
    John (son), 73, 74

Yew Tree Cottage, see No Name public house